FROM GOVERNMENT TO GOVERNANCE
A Brief Survey of the Indian Experience

Popular Social Science

FROM GOVERNMENT TO GOVERNANCE

A Brief Survey of the Indian Experience

KULDEEP MATHUR

nbt.india
एकः सूते सकलम्
NATIONAL BOOK TRUST, INDIA

ISBN 978-81-237-5410-9

First Edition 2008
Reprints 2009, 2010, 2011 (twice), 2013, 2015, 2016, 2018, 2020
(*Saka* 1942)

Published by the Director, National Book Trust, India
Nehru Bhawan, 5 Institutional Area, Phase-II
Vasant Kunj, New Delhi- 110 070
www.nbtindia.gov.in

Contents

Preface

Since the introduction of liberal economic policies in 1991, governance has emerged as an important element in policy discourse. Policy makers stress on governance reforms for improved policy outcomes. But the precise meaning of governance is not very clear. Different meanings lead to different thrusts in proposing and executing reform agenda. I am thankful to Prof. Bipan Chandra for giving me an opportunity to clarify some of these meanings and identify the various dimensions of change that are occurring in the domain of public institutions in India.

Kuldeep Mathur

Chapter I

Introduction: Emergence of the Concept of Governance

It is fair to say that until the late 1980s, governance was not a word heard frequently within the development community. Today it is a buzzword used freely in most publications emanating from government departments, donor agencies and academics. It is heavily relied upon to explain developmental outcomes. International and multilateral aid-giving agencies have adopted it as a general guiding principle to improve the capability of the recipient countries to handle development assistance better and utilise it more efficiently. Policymakers in countries now place stress on governance reforms for improved policy outcomes. However, improving a country's capability to utilise aid better or work for improved developmental performance does not connote the same meanings to everyone. The meanings range from following liberal economic policies, to strengthening and reforming market institutions, building capacities of public institutions to perform, encouraging democratic participation through strengthening civil society institutions etc. Some meanings are concerned with reducing the role of the state in economic activities, others with strengthening state institutions to promote the role of market and yet others relate to the encouragement of democracy and participation. The reason for this lack of consensus in its conceptual meaning and how it can be applied concretely lies in the way governance enters common parlance. The result is that multilateral aid-giving agencies choose different meanings to emphasise the intervention strategy they want to follow to bring about changes in the recipient countries. Governance entered the Western social science vocabulary after gaining prominence in the discourse of practitioners. But the use and meaning of the concept take different hues and these are influenced by the way the concept has risen and entered different discourses.

Ascendancy of the Concept

The rise in the popularity in the use of the term governance is closely linked with the redefinition of the role of state. In the post World War II period, state was seen as an engine of growth, but with failures in development performance, it began to be blamed for all that had gone wrong. Ineffective development policies and poor implementation of these policies together with inefficient and incompetent absorption of international aid, triggered the search for alternative frameworks for policy making and alternative institutions for delivering public services.

It is now widely known that governance was first used by the World Bank in its report on sub-Saharan Africa in 1989. In this report, the Bank suggested that the programmes of fiscal adjustment and investment in that region were being rendered ineffective by a 'crisis of governance.' What the Bank saw in its experience of advancing structural adjustment programmes was the weak role of the state and its institutions in implementing these programmes. There were incompetent and corrupt governments that tended to curtail or dilute these programmes and even after governments accepted the conditions, enjoined in these programs, they were not able to implement them. This led the Bank, in its initial formulation, to focus on managerial and administrative competence as a strategy to improve governance (World Bank, 1989; World Bank 1992) and committed itself to the seemingly more apolitical and largely technical strategy of improving governance. What was advocated was a slim but efficient administrative state, detached from its prior pervasive involvement in economic matters (Leftwich, 1994:368). The role of state was redefined in the World Development Report 1992 (4-11). The state could undertake basic investment in, and management of, essential social and physical infrastructure, but its central role was to encourage the free and fair play of market forces in an impartial, open and accountable manner.

What the World Bank did in redefining the state was to shift the focus from government to governance. But this shift reflected the ascendance of neo-liberal ideology in economic theory and public policy from the 1970s in the Western world. Many of these countries in the advanced world faced a fiscal crisis due to the inability to bear the burden of welfare policies and the cost of vast bureaucracies maintained to implement them. Consequently, social spending began to be reduced, market was increasingly relied upon to meet many demands of citizens and search for alternative strategies to deliver public services began. Privatization and liberalization became the new slogans of effective government. However, in this formulation, role of state was not reduced but reconceptualised. It was recognised that the liberal policies could only succeed in providing citizen welfare if the state had the capacity to direct and regulate them. Effective and competent bureaucracies were still needed but in different avatar.

This experience of advanced countries in redefining the

role of state was profoundly significant for the emerging conceptualization of governance and its use by the donor agencies. Neo-liberalism strengthens the social powers of capital especially finance capital and discourages state investments in sectors that can be included in the purview of the private sector. So the effect of the rise of the role of private enterprise or greater reliance on the market largely eclipsed the state oriented growth model that had been prevalent since the end of the Second World War. Governance now was envisaged in this new perspective and was not state centric. The state was one actor – albeit an important one—in steering society.

Together with this insistence of prioritization of markets in domestic public policies, processes of globalization further strengthened the role of financial capital and promoted its movement across countries. As more and more countries got incorporated in international production process, the demand of finance capital, as represented by transnational corporations, on the state was to provide conditions that would allow production to take place efficiently and smoothly. Good governance came to be associated with the capacity of the state to provide these conditions and create a climate that attracts international capital through corporations and aid through international agencies. The impact of the progress of globalization has thus been that of further emasculation of the role of state. The chief beneficiary of this development has undoubtedly been the domain of the market, which has gained previously unthinkable pre-eminence in the last decade of the twentieth century (Jayal, 2001:12).

Meanings of Governance

Reviews of the literature generally demonstrate that

governance has different meanings and is used in a variety of ways. But there is a baseline agreement that governance refers to the development of governing styles in which boundaries between and within public and private sectors have become blurred (Stoker, 1998:155). What previously were indisputably roles of government are now increasingly seen as more common generic, societal problems which can be resolved by political institutions but also by other actors. The main point is that political institutions no longer exercise a monopoly of the orchestration of governance (Pierre, 2000:4). The concept of governance indicates a shift away from well established notions of the way government sought to resolve social issues through top down approach.

In summarising the perspective of governance identified in the literature, Stoker (1998) lays down five dimensions. These dimensions are:

a. Governance refers to a complex set of institutions and actors that are drawn from but also beyond the government.
b. Governance recognises the blurring of boundaries and responsibilities for tackling social and economic issues.
c. Governance identifies the power dependence involved in the relationships between institutions involved in collective action.
d. Governance is about autonomous self-governing networks of actors.
e. Governance recognises the capacity to get things done which does not rest on the power of the government to command or use its authority. It sees government as able to use new tools and techniques to steer and guide.

More simply put, governance is concerned with network of relationships of three actors – state, market and civil society. It is an interactive process where government may like to impose its will but its acceptance will depend on compliance and action of others. One institution depends on another and this is what Stoker refers to as power dependence. In this relationships and networks, no one institution can easily dominate; it will depend on particular process of exchange. The monopoly of political institutions in providing services is diluted; the private sector and institutions of civil society fill in the space previously occupied by these institutions. New forms of institutions emerge and this finds expression in the blurring of boundaries between the public and the private sector. A range of voluntary agencies arise that respond to collective concerns.

Governance is concerned with the changes taking place in the organisation of the state and its relationships with private sector and civil society actors. Here academic attention turns from state-centric analysis towards an understanding of the wider public policy system in which the institutions of government appear to be involved in processes of negotiation, bargaining and compromise with a host of other actors. This is what is conventionally described as the transition from government to governance.

If academic attention in the perspective of governance shifts from a state-centric approach to a much broader complexity of institutions in the framing of public policy, the international agencies led by the World Bank have defined governance in a way that promotes neo-liberal policies. The World Bank defines governance as the institutional capacity of public organizations to provide the public and other goods demanded by a country's citizens in an effective, transparent, impartial and accountable manner, subject to resource constraints. This definition then supports the Bank's programmes in strengthening the institutional capacity in recipient governments so that governments are not only smaller but also better and more efficient.

This understanding entails four components of good governance that the World Bank has adopted as policy guidelines in recipient countries.

- Public sector management entails civil service reform and private sector initiatives.
- Legal framework for development is about making and enforcing rules that can make a market work, such as private property rights.
- Accountability aims at strengthening the institutions to hold the government accountable, as for example an ombudsman, the Auditor-General or parliamentary public accounts committee.
- Finally, transparency and information are key words for programmes that support a free media or help the government publicize statistics, such as publishing the public budget annually.

Operationally, the World Bank's notion of governance refers to reducing corruption and encouraging rule bound behaviour. In reforming public bureaucracies, it reflects the concerns of the Weberian model insisting on merit in recruitment, professionalization and neutrality and impartiality in enforcing rules. World Bank has employed six dimensions to construct measures of governance. These dimensions are:

- Voice and Accountability- measuring political, civil and human rights
- Instability and violence –measuring the likelihood of violent threats to or changes in government, including terrorism
- Government effectiveness- measuring the competence of the bureaucracy and the quality of public service delivery

- Regulatory burden- measuring the incidence of market-unfriendly policies
- Rule of law- measuring the quality of contract enforcement, the police, and the courts, as well as the likelihood of crime and violence
- Control of corruption-measuring the exercise of public power for private gain, including both petty and grand corruption and state capture.

World Bank has used perceptions of diverse categories of people of these dimensions to rank countries on good governance.

Even though the international aid giving agencies have now broadened their definition of governance, operational strategies are concerned with reforms in state institutions. This conception is based on efficiency criterion and demands improved state capacity to absorb aid and pursue developmental goals. Asian Development Bank, for example, has placed capacity building as the core dimension of its governance policy. But the capacity building exercise is to promote the role of the market and therefore includes thinning of bureaucracy and of reducing what is called overload of social spending on the state. It is in this perspective that the increased role of NGOs is envisaged as having state substituting capacities.

However, in the past decade or so, the enthusiasm for the market has become subdued and there has been greater concern expressed for establishing institutions that can respond to its vagaries. Development economists have come to recognize that good governance is not merely a matter of promoting markets or encouraging private investment. Stable political regimes, appropriate legal framework, conducive social institutions and social values also matter. Democracy is valuable in this context for it provides legitimation for good governance (Hirst, 2000). But democracy does not mean the existence of formal institutions of periodic elections and political parties alone. It also means that the substance of democracy is also valued. This comes through with increased participation of people in the use and management of resources through greater decentralization, sharing power and greater responsiveness of the government to issues of equity and justice.

In concluding this section, it is necessary to remind ourselves that the concept of governance reflects empirical reality much more sharply than what focus on government alone did. It points to networks in society that are involved in policy making and moves away from the well established notions of authoritative single agencies at work. Networks connect disparate set of actors who jointly realize that they need one another to craft effective political agreements. Their efforts to find solutions acceptable to all who are involved tend to challenge the constitutional institutions established for this purpose (see Hajer and Wagenaar (ed) 2003). Thus, governance provides a new perspective and provides the potential to explore how power shifts take place in society. Governance now is envisaged in this new perspective and is not state centric. The state is one actor – albeit an important one – in steering society.

The challenge for the practitioners and international aid agencies is the realization that governance is not confined to civil service reform or introduction of corporate practices in government alone. Reform for good governance carries a wide agenda that touches virtually every aspect of politics, economy and society. The governance agenda is particularly demanding of states that are poor, disorganized, vulnerable to political disruption and lacking in legitimacy (Grindle,2004). The most important realization that has emerged in the efforts at external initiatives of reform in governance is that this reform is a matter of political contestation. Without political commitment even the technical strategy of building institutional capacities cannot work. Each country has its own history and context. There is no universal model of good governance. It is good to remind ourselves of an old lesson learnt during the heydays of development administration movement when strengthening bureaucratic capacities was the order of day: '...decision-making is enmeshed so intricately and so deeply in the surrounding culture that it cannot be extricated as an autonomous behavior and transplanted' (Braibanti, 1966:165).

More simply put, governance is concerned with network of relationships of three actors – state, market and civil society. It is an interactive process where government may like to impose its will but its acceptance will depend on compliance and action of others. One institution depends on another and this is what Stoker refers to as power dependence. In this relationships and networks, no one institution can easily dominate; it will depend on particular process of exchange. The monopoly of political institutions in providing services is diluted; the private sector and institutions of civil society fill in the space previously occupied by these institutions. New forms of institutions emerge and this finds expression in the blurring of boundaries between the public and the private sector. A range of voluntary agencies arise that respond to collective concerns.

Use of the term in India

The term governance gained currency in India with the liberalization of the Indian economy in 1991. The decade of the 90s saw increasing use of the term 'governance' to explain the failures of development and the policy makers accepted that governance is critical to the alleviation of poverty in the country. During the period preceding this decade, the discussion of failures of the planned strategy of development, particularly in the achievements of the various Five Year Plans, usually veered around the impediments created by the inherited bureaucratic and administrative system of the British colonial days. The governmental response to these concerns was to focus on administrative reform. Even when these reforms did not succeed to make effective changes, the Plans continued to emphasize the role of administration in Plan performance.[1]

It was the Eighth Five Year Plan (1992-1997) that pointed out the need to re-examine and to reorient the role of the government as well as the process of planning. In this re-orientation, the Plan indicated that while there may have been good reasons in the past for the public sector to take the initiative in industrial areas where the private sector would ordinarily either not enter or hesitate to do so, such reasons do not exist today. Therefore, restructuring of public sector would essentially entail vacating such areas for private sector initiatives. Second, addressing itself to the task of people's involvement in development, the Plan emphasized that the role of the government should be to create right type of institutional infrastructure so that people participate more

---

1. The Second and Third Five Year Plans carried full chapters on the role of administration in the strategy of planned economic development.

fully. It referred to the increasing role of voluntary agencies, panchayats and cooperatives.

Thus began the journey of governance discourse in India but not entirely without the influence from the West and the agenda of donor agencies. The Tenth Plan (2002-2007) explicitly took upon the issue of governance by indicating that governance has in the recent times emerged at the forefront of the development agenda and good governance is one of the most crucial factors required if the targets of the Tenth Plan are to be achieved. The Plan then went on to define governance as the management of all such processes that, in any society, define the environment which permits and enables individuals to raise their capability levels, on one hand, and provide opportunities to realise their potential and enlarge the set of available choices, on the other. The Approach Paper to the 11th Five Year Plan took this concern further by arguing that 'all our efforts to achieve rapid and inclusive development will come to naught, if we cannot ensure good governance in the manner public programmes are implemented and, equally in the way government interacts with the ordinary citizen.' Having emphasized the importance of good governance, the Paper goes on to add:

> Corruption is now seen to be endemic in all spheres and this problem needs to be addressed urgently. Better design of projects and implementation mechanisms and procedures can reduce the scope for corruption. Much more needs to be done by the Centre and the States to reduce the discretionary power of the government, ensure greater transparency and accountability, and create awareness among citizens....

Indian policy makers see corruption as the most endemic

and entrenched manifestation of poor governance in India. Planning Commission in its National Human Development Report (2002:122) sees corruption embedded in the way government activities were being carried on in the country. The institutional arrangements in regulating the economy were such that state officials had monopoly as well as discretionary powers vested in them. The problem was compounded by procedural and legal hurdles that an individual had to confront in almost every interface with public authorities. It suggests that the solution to the problem does not lie merely in deregulation and liberalization of the economy. Systematic efforts have to be made to review prevalent institutional arrangements and accountability mechanisms have to be strengthened for those who hold power.

The emphasis of the Planning Commission in improving governance in the country is on building state capacities, strengthening public service delivery mechanisms and creating effective institutions for decentralization. The National Human Development Report (2002:124) lays down the following agenda:

- Devolution of power to manage local affairs and decentralization of decision-making;
- Civil service reform aimed at improving transparency, accountability efficiency and sensitivity in public administration at all levels;
- Enforcing incentive/disincentive structures that truly reflect social values and norms;
- Procedural reforms covering all aspects of government's interface with public; and
- Empowerment, particularly of women, the marginal and the excluded.

However, the agenda for good governance is very long and complex. As Grindle (2004:525-26) points out, good governance is deeply problematic as a guide to development. Getting good governance calls for improvements that touch virtually all aspects of the public sector—from institutions that set the rules of the game for economic and political interaction, to decision-making structures that determine priorities among public problems and allocate resources to respond to them, to organizations that manage administrative systems and deliver goods and services to citizens, to human resources that staff government bureaucracies, to the interface of officials and citizens in political and bureaucratic arenas. Getting good governance at times implies changes in political organization, the representation of interests, and processes for public debate and policy decision making.

Reforms are essentially a political activity. They are political whether in the sphere of liberalizing the economy and deregulating it or in designing institutions that emerge as the state transforms itself in the perspective of neo-liberal policies. As we see in the pages that follow, good intentions are not enough and therefore getting good governance has been a major challenge.

Chapter II Constitutional Institutions of Governance

Within the governance perspective, state continues to occupy a pre-eminent position in re-structuring relationships in society. State exercises power through a diversity of institutions. It legitimizes itself by the way these institutions function. Therefore, it is important to analyse the way these state institutions perform and how they have responded to the new demands of governance. India gave itself a constitution that laid down a framework of institutions that govern the country. A constitution provides coherence to institutions and establishes what are known as the rules of the game. This coherence is provided by the way functions and responsibilities are assigned to them and relationships among them are delineated. However, not all institutions perform as expected of them and not all of them relate to each other in a coherent manner. There are many reasons for this but it is important to realize that state gains legitimacy and carries out tasks of development on the basis of performance of these institutions (Kapur and Mehta, ed. 2005).

The Constitution of India was passed by the Constituent Assembly of India on November 26, 1949, and came into effect on January 26, 1950. That is why the date of the promulgation of the Constitution is celebrated as the Republic Day. The Constitution lays down the basic structure of government under which the people are to be governed. It establishes the main organs of government the executive, the legislature and the judiciary. The Constitution not only defines the powers of each organ, but also demarcates their responsibilities. It regulates the relationship between the different organs and between the government and the people. All laws have to conform to the Constitution and to the its Amendments as incorporated from time to time. There have been 93 amendments to the Constitution till 2003.

The Constituent Assembly had been elected for the undivided India in 1946. The work on framing the Constitution began after independence when the Muslim League members had left for Pakistan. No new members were added to replace them. The members were elected by provincial legilatures that had been elected through a limited franchise. Members from the princely states were selected through mutual consultation. The Drafting Committee was chaired by Dr. Ambedkar. The Constitution is a lengthy document consisting of 370 articles and 10 schedules. It may be summarised as having three strands: protecting and enhancing national unity and integrity; establishing the institutions and spirit of democracy; and fostering a social revolution to better the lot of mass of Indians (Austin, 2003:6).

Broadly, the Constitution provided for a federal framework with a parliamentary system of government based on the Westminster model. The President is the Head of State while the Prime Minister is the head of government. Governor and the Chief Ministers are similar functionaries at the state level. There are two Houses of Parliament – one Lok Sabha that is directly elected by the people and the second – Rajya Sabha elected indirectly by the state legislatures and with some nominated members. Unlike the US Senate, the number elected by states depends on the size of their population. The legislative jurisdiction is determined by the provision of three lists –central, state and concurrent lists. There is a unified judiciary rising from State High Courts to Supreme Court at the national level. There are subordinate courts at the district level and below administered by the States. The Constitution then goes on to provide for Fundamental Rights and non-justiciable Directive Principles of State Policy. Many other institutions that are concerned with other facets of citizens' life as well as those that help in coordinating government's activities were created.

Constitution is the formal framework of institutions and relationships that was adopted by the people of India to govern themselves. The way this mosaic unfolds in real life determines the quality of governance in the country. Good governance is when the functioning of institutions in a web of relationships leads to development. However, institutions do not work on their own but are worked by individuals who shape these institutions and© help forge relations among them. Dr. Ambedkar is quoted as saying: 'If the Constitution of India gets derailed, the reason will not be that we had a bad Constitution. What we will have to say is that man was vile'. Constitution lays down what is expected of these institutions; actual performance shows whether these expectations have been fulfilled or not. The rest of the chapter examines the performance of some of the constitutional macro-institutions of government and attempts to analyze the way they have fulfilled their constitutional obligations.

India's Federal Structure

India consists of 28 states, and seven what are known as "Union Territories". Of the seven, two Union Territories (Delhi and Pondicherry) have their own elected legislatures whereas the remaining ones are governed directly by appointees of the center. The states replicate the Centre in terms of governing institutions. The powers between the Centre and the States are constitutionally assigned through Schedule VII. In many ways, the division of powers gives pre-eminence to the Centre making the federation lean towards a unitary system. The exact nature of the division of powers, and how that has played out in practice, determines the extent of centralization within this federal system. In addition, the size of the states also has implications for this characterization. Political parties play a major in role in the interactions that take place between the Centre and the State. For a long time the same political party ruled at the Centre and most of the States reducing differences between the two. But as divergence grew, conflicts have increasingly come to the fore. Different parties ruling neighbouring states have also fuelled tensions on issues that could have been resolved through negotiations and bargains. In addition, the nature of political parties themselves, have an influence on the way the federal system works. The rise of regional parties and their inclusion as coalition partners in central governments has made regional demands more strident.

A perennial source of dissatisfaction with the federal relations has been the division of financial powers between the Centre and the States. The States have felt that the power of raising resources is not commensurate with the development responsibilities given to them. In addition, over the course of years, a feeling has been generated that the distribution of fiscal resources has not always been fair. Political biases have influenced the amounts distributed and many states have felt deprived and blamed the Centre for their lack of development.

The Constitution in its Seventh Schedule assigned major role of development to the states with subjects like agriculture, public health, education, irrigation, fisheries, land rights, industries etc. The states were also given the responsibility of maintaining law and order with police under their jurisdiction. These subjects require considerable expenditures; the source of taxation is limited to tax on sale and purchase of goods. Another problem is that states have large bureaucracies to implement the development programmes and their salary and wage bills keeps on rising as the Centre revises salaries and wages for its own bureaucracies. The post-economic reform period has seen increasing state budget deficits particularly after the recommendations of the Fifth Pay Commission were implemented by the Central government for its employees. The Sixth Pay Commission has been appointed in 2006 and some states have already expressed their fears of further deterioration in their financial condition.

The Constitution recognized that the States will have limited funds and the Centre may face political challenges in distributing resources to them. It provided for a Finance Commission to determine the share of taxes between the Centre and the states and also to recommend the principles that would govern the grants-in-aid from the Consolidated Fund of India. These Finance Commissions are appointed every five years by the President of India; their recommendations have been usually accepted by the Government.

Another source of funds for the States is the Planning Commission. There has been no provision for plan transfers in the Constitution but as there was a stress on planned economic development, the central government began to channel what were called plan funds under the provisions of

Art. 282 of the Constitution. These Plan funds are distributed under what is known as the Gadgil formula which is agreed to by the states in the National Development Council.[2] Planning Commission develops a five-year-plan indicating investments for each sector of the economy and each state. With this as background, the states work out their respective annual plans for each year based on their own estimates of resource available. The state plans are then approved by the Planning Commission. What determines the state plans is their own estimate of resources available to them, the resources transferred under the Gadgil formula merely supplements these resources.

In addition, central ministries have continued to feel the need to transfer funds to the states to influence their priorities of expenditure through what have come to be known as centrally sponsored schemes. Funds channeled through these schemes are not subject to any formula but depend on the discretion of the Ministries concerned. Currently, there are around 155 centrally sponsored schemes with an allocation of around Rs71996 crores this fiscal. Since the Fourth Plan (1969-74) two significant features of central transfers of funds have emerged. One is that there has been an increase in the discretionary component of transfers. Second, within statutory transfers, the proportion of tax devolution, which had already been high, has increased, while that of grants has declined (Rao and Singh, 2003:368).

The more controversial of central government transfers are funds provided through centrally sponsored schemes.

2. The National Development Council is chaired by the Prime Minister and its members include all the Cabinet ministers, Chief Ministers of the states and all members of the Planning Commission. It was set up to approve the Fiver Year Plans.

States have seen these schemes as political efforts to win constituencies by party in power at the Centre. States have also seen them as encroachment on the development functions and responsibilities given to them under the federal system. Since the policies of liberalization were adopted, centrally sponsored schemes assumed even greater importance for the central government which started getting international funds for specific purposes. The centre wanted to monitor the utilization of the funds itself rather than leave it to the states. The controversies arise due to the fact that non-economic considerations enter their design, location and implementation. These schemes have acted as one of the major irritants in centre-state relations from a long time. Apart from this, these schemes have languished because of inadequate commitment by the states responsible for their implementation. The issue has been taken up by several committees and commissions and the demand for curtailing these schemes is again being considered as the 11th Five Year Plan (2007-12) is being framed.[3]

The President is empowered to establish an inter-State Council to resolve disputes and discuss matters of common interest in another Constitutional provision incorporated in Art. 263. While several subject specific consultative forums like Central Council of Health or a Transport Council had

---

3. It has been reported that Planning Commission Deputy Chairman has met Finance Minister on the issue of restructuring of centrally-sponsored schemes. The Finance Minister expressed willingness to have a re-look on the policy governing Centrally sponsored programmes in order that State Governments get funds to finance locally relevant schemes. Both sides have already agreed on restructuring of the schemes and curtailing the subsidy bill, Ahluwalia told reporters after the meeting. (*Hindu Businessline*, July 21, 2006)

been established earlier, an all embracing Inter-State Council was established only in 1990 on the recommendation of the Sarkaria Commission. This Council is chaired by the Prime Minister and consists of Prime Minister; Chief Ministers of all States, Chief Ministers of Union territories having a Legislative Assembly and Administrators of Union territories not having a Legislative Assembly; and six Ministers of Cabinet rank in the Union Council of Ministers to be nominated by the Prime Minister. This Council has a secretariat to organise meetings and prepare background papers for discussion.

The centralizing features of the Indian federal framework have come under attack particularly after the rise of regional parties at the helm of governments in the states and the breakdown of Congress hegemony. In 1983, Chief Ministers of Karnataka, Andhra, Tamil Nadu and Pondicherry got together in a conclave.[4] The four Chief Ministers decided to form a council of southern chief ministers, so they could settle the problems at their own level (Austin, 2003:542). Mrs. Indira Gandhi, the then Prime minister, responded by announcing a commission to study inter-state relations and make recommendations. This commission was chaired by a retired Judge of the Supreme Court Justice RS Sarkaria[5]. Many of the issues that were taken up for consideration have continued to rankle the relationships till today long after recommendations were made in 1990 when the Report was made public. Undoubtedly some issues have receded to the background because of changed political context but others

4. The Chief minister of Kerala was from the Congress party and did not join the meeting.
5. Though popularly known as Sarkaria Commission officially it was known as Commission on Centre-State Relations.(1989)

remain, particularly those in the realm of financial and administrative relations.

The federal system as it worked before liberal economic reforms were introduced is facing a transformation. The states are seen competing for foreign direct investment and pursuing their projects independently of the Centre. Chief Ministers are travelling abroad seeking opportunities of trade and business and soliciting multinationals and Non-Resident Indians to invest in their states. Maharashtra was among the first states that attracted Enron, a US corporation to invest for power generation. It persuaded the government of India to accept many clauses in the contract that were ambiguous and ultimately contradictory interpretations of these clauses led to the abrogation of the contract. Both Andhra Pradesh and Karnataka have been in the forefront of inviting multilateral funding for projects in their states (Rudolphs, 2001). The impact of economic reforms has also been uneven on states. Some states stand to gain greater benefit in a liberalized economy and hence support reforms at the Centre. This breaks the earlier consensus among states of joint pleas for more central funds and at the same time gives greater freedom to states to use their own strategies to raise resources (see Jenkins 1999). The argument rests more on the ability of the states to deregulate and liberalise rather than on what the central government can do for them.

The Executive

The President is head of state and all governmental action is taken in his name. He is elected by an electoral college consisting of all elected members of both Houses and Parliament and elected members of the Legislative assemblies of the States. His tenure of office is for five years. Following the Westminster model, the President is only a nominal head of the executive and is supposed to exercise his powers on the 'aid and advise' of the Council of Ministers headed by the Prime Minister. Usually, the Presidents have not asserted their own power over that of the advice of the Prime Minister in Council but there have been differences between the President and the Prime Minister (Manor, 1994). As a matter of fact, President Fakrauddin Ali Ahmed was seen as being too compliant when he readily signed the proclamation of emergency brought in by Prime Minister Indira Gandhi in 1975.

The inability of the Presidents to assert their views was partly influenced by the fact that the advice came from council of ministers elected by single party majorities in parliament. After 1989, the situation changed when no single party commanded a majority and coalitions became the order of the day. Manor (2005) points out that President Narayanan chose to strike a different path when he asked the Gujral government to reconsider the advice to impose President's rule in Uttar Pradesh in 1998. On reconsideration the government did not pursue the issue. He also stepped in to ask the BJP to seek a vote of confidence in Parliament in 1999 when it seemed to have lost its majority.[6]

It must be said to the credit of the strength of the parliamentary system that there have been no case where the

6. Manor (2003: 121) finds President Narayanan most assertive of the Presidents who served after 1989. He has suggested that his assertiveness is not only explained by hung parliaments but his ideas of legitimacy. He believed that government has come to be perceived as insufficiently responsive and inclusive. There is thus need to find ways to open government upto previously excluded groups, to ensure that diversity is respected, and to seek greater synergy between state and society.

differences between the President and the Prime Minister have stalled the functioning of the system. There were hints of differences between the President and the party in power during 1999-2004 and currently between 2004 and now in 2006 but they have been smoothly tided over without any confrontation taking place (see for illustrations Manor, 2005).

Prime Minister and the Council of Ministers

If the President is Head of state, Prime Minister is Head of government. Nominally appointed by the President, Prime Minister is the leader of the majority party in the Parliament. The President has little discretion in the choice. However, in recent years, the President has had to act with caution because many times majorities are under dispute and the President has to act in a way that the majorities are proven and transparent. The ministers are clearly appointed by the President on the advice of the Prime Minister. Dropping or dismissing a minister from the cabinet is a virtual power in the hands of the Prime Minister and the President is bound by his or her advice. The Prime Minister, on the other hand, loses office if he or she loses her majority in the Parliament.

Under Art. 74(1), all the powers and functions vested in the President are to be exercised on the advice of the Prime Minister and her cabinet. The question that has been raised often is whether the President is bound by the advice of the Prime Minister in all matters. The question was raised by the President very early in the life of the Constitution when, in 1960, President Rajendra Prasad observed: 'There is no provision in the Constitution which in so many words lays down that President shall be bound to act in accordance with the advice of the Council of Ministers.' When the issue was raised in the Supreme Court, its interpretation was that the President was a figure-head and had to work like the British Crown. This question was put beyond political controversy under the 42nd Amendment of the Constitution when Art. 74 (1) was substituted thus: 'There shall be a Council of Ministers with Prime Minister at the head to aid and advise the President who shall in the exercise of his functions, act in accordance with such advice.' Though the President still has the right to send back cabinet recommendation for reconsideration he has to accept it once it is returned.

Members of the cabinet are the team convened by the Prime Minister for collective decision-making. They are also ministers in charge of specific ministries or portfolios with responsibility for the effective performance of all departments under them. Ministers thus have a dual role – one as a member of a political collectivity and the other as efficient managers of complex organizations. One would expect a Prime Minister to seek qualities of both kinds when choosing a cabinet. In addition, it is also assumed that cabinet ministers would provide independent view-points but would nevertheless implement whatever is collectively agreed.

Usually, the Prime Ministers have asserted their leadership such that independent opinions are not commonly encouraged. Very early in the history of cabinet functioning in India, conflicts surfaced between cabinet ministers and the Prime Minister. As Home Minister, Patel once wrote to Nehru deploring the latter's tendency to interfere in ministerial affairs. Patel said that ministers should be free to carry out cabinet decisions and that the Prime Minister should step in only when the disputes rose. Nehru countered that it was his responsibility to maintain the utmost co-ordination which would not be possible if ministers took important decisions without reference to the Prime Minister or the cabinet. Patel died soon thereafter and Nehru's interpretation became accepted practice. This convention was taken to its logical end by Indira Gandhi whose cabinets were reduced to a collection of 'tame subordinates' and the government became a 'one-man show'. A former Secretary to the Prime Minister has described how members of her cabinets produced only such proposals as would find favour with Mrs Gandhi (Alexander 1991). Short tenures and rapid turnover of cabinet ministers have also helped to accentuate this process.

However, the notion of collective responsibility is explicitly recognised in a parliamentary system of government. But the Prime Minister's prerogative to appoint his own cabinet does not, however, give him unlimited freedom to do so. The reason is the nature of the parliamentary system in which it is the political party that comes into power and not an individual. The cabinet is the instrument of the party or what can be called its government wing; when the government performs well, the credit basically goes to the party of which it is a part. It is the government record that makes or unmakes victory in the elections. Hence, the party is very interested in how the cabinet behaves and functions and who its members are. It expects that only those will gain entry into the cabinet who can faithfully represent views and carry out its manifestos.

Choosing a cabinet presents a greater challenge when a single political party does not get a majority and the largest party may have to cobble up a coalition to either fight elections to gain a majority or after election bargain with other parties for support. In both cases, those who actually become cabinet ministers are nominees of the coalition partners. In such cases, ministers sense of collective responsibility may not always be the kind demanded by system.[7] Many different forces operate to constrain collective decision-making. Some are due to decisions being taken elsewhere than in the cabinet. Others stem from public perceptions that associate collective decisions with conflict; it is "bad" for the cabinet to appear conflictual, at least frequently. Thus a cabinet is a collective only formally. Its collective character is constrained by the party parameters or by Prime Ministerial ambitions.

Members of the cabinet are the team convened by the Prime Minister for collective decision-making. They are also ministers in charge of specific ministries or portfolios with responsibility for the effective performance of all departments under them. Ministers thus have a dual role – one as a member of a political collectivity and the other as efficient managers of complex organizations. Ministers are also playing another role: that of being members of the coalition partner. One would expect a Prime Minister to seek qualities that subserve to the role of being member of the collective rather than assert the views of the party to which the Minister belongs when choosing a cabinet. Increasingly, Ministers representing party views are signaling a change in the working of the cabinet as a collectivity. The fragility of coalitions is also giving space to parties critical for sustaining a majority but sparse in representation to hold many collective decisions to ransom.

---

7. During the tenure of Atal Behari Vajpayee, Shiv Sena, an important coalition partner had nominated Mr. Suresh Prabhu to the cabinet. He was then withdrawn and replaced by another party member. The Prime Minister had little say in this and accepted the new nominee. The new incumbent said, "If Mr Thackeray thinks he should give me anything more important I will take it as an honour." Mr Geete did not fail to mention that every Shiv Sena member obeyed what Mr Thackeray said. see *Tribune*, August 21, 2002.

But it is assumed that cabinet ministers would provide independent view-points but would nevertheless implement whatever is collectively agreed.

The Legislature

The Constitution has provided for two Houses of Parliament. Lok Sabha is directly elected by the people and each member of the Lok Sabha represents a constituency of 550,000 to 750,000 people. The Rajya Sabha is composed of 250 members of whom 12 are nominated by the President and the rest elected by the state legislatures as representatives of states and union territories. The normal term of the Lok Sabha is five years and the Rajya Sabha is not subject to dissolution. Its members are elected for six years and a third of its members retire every two years.

In most countries there has been a decline of legislatures. The cabinet and the bureaucracy have gradually eroded the significance of parliament. A prime ministerial system of government seems to be replacing what was traditionally known as the parliamentary one. In the early period of independence, Nehru took special care to give prestige to the parliament by attending its sessions regularly, initiating major policy debates and admonishing members to keep up the dignity of the House. This concern gradually diminished with even the Prime Ministers' attendance of sessions going down. Parliament also began to spend less time on critical matters of policy and budget. The parliament has increasingly devoted more time to political issues. But this time has increasingly been occupied more by confrontation than debate. People have been treated to unseemly behaviour of the members of parliament physically fighting with colleagues, drowning other people's voices or flouting the ruling of the presiding officers. What was possible on the streets has becom possible on the floor of the House. The result has been that during the period 1985 to 1995 discussions on the financial approvals of only a few ministries – seven to be specific- have been taken up. The Demands for Grants for as many as 11 ministries were not taken up for detailed discussion even once and most of the time more than 85% of the Budget was passed without any discussion (Shastri, 1998:185-86).

In view of this trend, the Parliament decided to set up Standing Committees for most ministries in 1993. These committees consist of members from both Houses of Parliament and chairs are chosen by proportional party representation. Usually highly regarded parliamentarians are chosen to lead the committees even if they belong to the opposition. Every committee has a maximum of 45 members and each Member of Parliament serves a two-year term on at least one committee.

The objective was that this would provide for an opportunity for detailed discussions of the financial proposals and also give the members of parliament an occasion to give more considered opinion on the policy issues as suggested through the proposed budget. The committees were designed to be a mechanism that would provide meaningful dialogue between the government and members of Parliament. A system was established so that the legislators could consider matters of a technical nature that Parliament, as a whole could not take time to discuss. Continuous legislative oversight would ostensibly be produced in a setting where there was a constant turnover as the committees could avail themselves of the testimony of expert witnesses, initiate studies, issue reports, and examine draft legislation as a prelude to legislative action or postponement (Rubinoff, 1996:727).

Despite the establishment of these committees, legislators are dissatisfied with the way that they can influence the government. Rubinoff (1996) interviewed a large number of Parliamentarians who felt that the resources they had at their disposal to perform their tasks were inadequate compared to those available to the executive branch. For the most part, there has been inadequate time for the new committees to prepare in-depth studies. This led to perfunctory reports not taken seriously by the government or the media. Another significant issue pointed out by Rubinoff (1996) is that there is no incentive for the ministers to take the new committees seriously as long as they do not have to testify before them. With sessions closed to the public and only secretaries (civil servants heading the ministries) required to appear, there is no reason for busy cabinet ministers to participate in committee activities. Since they were not confirmed by the legislature and enjoy permanency of tenure through constitutional provisions, the secretaries who appear are not directly accountable to the parliamentary system. The legislators unable to fall back on alternative sources of ideas or policy are overwhelmed by the arguments put forward by the bureaucrats. For all these reasons, the committees have not been able to perform an effective role in policy making.

The responsibility of the legislature does not stop at approving the financial outlays at the start of the year. It is also important for the legislature to examine, after the financial year is over, with the help of the audit reports prepared by the Comptroller and Auditor General of India, if public money was spent according to its intentions and whether there was any waste, fraud or misuse. The work of the Public Accounts Committee and the Committee on Public Undertakings relies on the audit reports to examine this part of the government activity. These committees have always been considered as important pillars of democracy and its watchdogs. Unfortunately, this examination is also not taken seriously and is delayed by several years. 'As far as it has been possible to find out, the central Public Accounts Committee has not yet given its report about even the Bofors audit which is sometimes credited with bringing down the government of Rajiv Gandhi' (Joseph, 2000:2999). The financial irregularities that the CAG points out neither catch the attention of the parliamentarians or of the media.

An important bottleneck for members of parliament in taking cognizance of policy ideas coming from diverse sources is the fact that there is no provision of research staff to give them support to identify important issues. Only those issues that are politically volatile and visible tend to catch their attention. This lack of expertise available to the members of Parliament has affected the working of the new committee system that has been adopted in 1993. Among political parties in India, tradition of strong research cells to support the legislative activities of its representatives is weak. Parliament has a rudimentary staff that can collect relevant data or refer to important sources. There is a well-equipped library but the actual research or drawing policy implications from data available has to be done by the members of the Parliament themselves. Not many are inclined to do so and most do not have the capability even if they may have the inclination. The result is that these committees fall short of the role that Congressional committees play in US even if they are modeled after them. The tendency to pick up politically visible issues or those that will find prominent place in the media becomes strong. Discussions in the Parliament or in the committees are bereft of policy concerns. (see Mathur and Jayal, 1993 for discussion on drought policy in Parliament and Jain, 1995 for similar discussion on electronics policy).

In general, Parliament has lost its sheen. There is general apathy among its members towards parliamentary work, absenteeism among members has assumed alarming proportions and defections for money and office have been a common phenomenon (Kashyap, 2000:138). Frequently debates turn into unruly fighting matches and pandemonium prevails on the floor of the House. The result is that the role of the Parliament as a body that seeks to influence government policy on the basis of it being the voice of the people has suffered considerably. The representatives also do not come from a background that reflects these urges. It is important to point out that the political parties also do not prepare them for this policy role. The parties do not have any research organization that can frame alternative points of view. It is left to the individuals to search for such opinions from professionals and academics that they may know or who are able to invite them to seminars and discussions. Most of such inputs are of ad hoc nature and are generated only through personal volition. The result is that the members of Parliament have rarely demanded research support; more committed among them use the well-equipped parliamentary library or avail of the services of its professional staff.

Another reason why parliamentarians do not demand research support is that they do not consider their role as a lawmaker as very important. The constituency demands are so strong that they can ignore them only at the peril of losing next elections. The constituency sees its MP as an intermediary sorting out all kinds of difficulties between the constituents and the authorities that provide those services.

These may range from municipal problems, to getting employment, or even helping to jump the queue in getting air and rail tickets, or gas or telephone connection. As Surya Prakash (1995:50) says 'The MP may be an acknowledged authority on constitutional law, foreign relations or defense. But this will hardly please his constituents. The clogged drains and bad roads will, in all probability seal his fate.'

If the committees of Parliament, on the whole, serve a limited purpose in ensuring accountability of the government, a more informal and perhaps more useful avenue of accountability might be seen in the form of questions that MPs pose to the government during the first hour of each meeting (Agarwal, 2005:93). The number of questions asked has increased enormously in the last five decades; the figure of 50,000 questions in oral and written form that were allowed in the first parliament has doubled in the 11th Parliament. Ultimately, the extent to which Parliament can hold executive accountable depends on the strength of the Opposition and the level of informed debate.[8]

The ability of Parliament in providing good governance has also got limited by several other factors. One is that the character of representation has visibly changed. Criminalization of politics has been under discussion for quite sometime and now increasingly so because a large number of politicians who get elected as Members of Parliament have criminal records. There are now around 20% of MPs who attract varying degree of penalties under the Indian Penal Code (Behar et.al. eds 2006). The Lok Sabha in its special

8. Jayal (2007) has argued that "the briefest moment of reflection on our political debates will reveal a polarization based on prejudice masquerading as opinion and opinion masquerading as argument."

session to commemorate the Golden Jubilee of Indian independence on 31 August 1997 resolved: 'That more especially all political parties shall undertake all such steps as will attain the objectives of ridding our polity of criminalization of politics.' The Election Commission is also seized of the issue but under the law a person is disqualified from standing for election only on conviction by the court of law, which does not take place so easily (ibid:20).

Another is that parliament is allowing itself less and less time to perform its traditional functions. The fourteenth Lok Sabha, that began its term in June 2004, continues to show increasing challenge in finding time to discuss and debate legislative issues. With political competition intensifying over the years, no opportunity is lost by the political parties to put its opposing group in the dock. There has not only been a decline in the number of days that Parliament has its sittings but also when on the days it meets much time is lost due to interruptions leaving very little time for laid down business of the House. Consequently, the list of bills pending for approval keeps lengthening and private members literally have no opportunity to table their proposals. Even those that are tabled get little time for discussion; to the extent that the Central budgets are being approved in record times of less than half-hour.

The Supreme Court

One of the unique features of the Indian Constitution is that, notwithstanding the adoption of a federal system and existence of Central Acts and State Acts in their respective spheres, it has generally provided for a single integrated system of Courts to administer both Union and State laws. At the apex of the entire judicial system, exists the Supreme Court of India below which is the High Courts in each State or group of States. Below the High Courts lie a hierarchy of Subordinate Courts. Panchayat Courts also function in some States under various names like Nyaya Panchayat, Panchayat Adalat, Gram Kachheri, etc. to decide civil and criminal disputes of petty and local nature. Different State laws provide for different kinds of jurisdiction of courts. Each State is divided into judicial districts presided over by a District and Sessions Judge, which is the principal civil court of original jurisdiction and can try all offences including those punishable with death. The Sessions Judge is the highest judicial authority in a district. Below him, there are Courts of civil jurisdiction, known in different States as Munsifs, Sub-Judges, Civil Judges and the like. Similarly, the criminal judiciary comprises the Chief Judicial Magistrates and Judicial Magistrates of First and Second Class.

The original Constitution of 1950 envisaged a Supreme Court with a Chief Justice and 7 puisne Judges - leaving it to Parliament to increase this number. In the early years, all the Judges of the Supreme Court sat together to hear the cases presented before them. As the work of the Court increased and arrears of cases began to cumulate, Parliament increased the number of Judges from 8 in 1950 to 11 in 1956, 14 in 1960, 18 in 1978 and 26 in 1986. As the number of the Judges has increased, they sit in smaller Benches of two and three - coming together in larger Benches of 5 and more only when required to do so or to settle a difference of opinion or controversy.

The Supreme Court of India comprises the Chief Justice and not more than 25 other Judges appointed by the President of India. Supreme Court Judges retire upon attaining the age of 65 years. In order to be appointed as a Judge of the Supreme

Court, a person must be a citizen of India and must have been, for at least five years, a Judge of a High Court or of two or more such Courts in succession, or an Advocate of a High Court or of two or more such Courts in succession for at least 10 years or he must be, in the opinion of the President, a distinguished jurist. Provisions exist for the appointment of a Judge of a High Court as an Ad-hoc Judge of the Supreme Court and for retired Judges of the Supreme Court or High Courts to sit and act as Judges of that Court.

The Constitution seeks to ensure the independence of Supreme Court Judges in various ways. A Judge of the Supreme Court cannot be removed from office except by an order of the President passed after an address in each House of Parliament supported by a majority of the total membership of that House and by a majority of not less than two-thirds of members present and voting, and presented to the President in the same Session for such removal on the ground of proved misbehaviour or incapacity. A person who has been a Judge of the Supreme Court is debarred from practicing in any court of law or before any other authority in India.

The Supreme Court has original, appellate and advisory jurisdiction. Its exclusive original jurisdiction extends to any dispute between the Government of India and one or more States or between the Government of India and any State or States on one side and one or more States on the other or between two or more States, if and insofar as the dispute involves any question (whether of law or of fact) on which the existence or extent of a legal right depends. In addition, Article 32 of the Constitution gives an extensive original jurisdiction to the Supreme Court in regard to enforcement of Fundamental Rights. It is empowered to issue directions, orders or writs, including writs in the nature of habeas corpus, mandamus, prohibition, quo warranto and certiorari to enforce them.

The appellate jurisdiction of the Supreme Court can be invoked by a certificate granted by the High Court concerned under Article 132(1), 133(1) or 134 of the Constitution in respect of any judgment, decree or final order of a High Court in both civil and criminal cases, involving substantial questions of law as to the interpretation of the Constitution.

The Supreme Court has special advisory jurisdiction in matters which may specifically be referred to it by the President of India under Article 143 of the Constitution.

Judiciary and the Supreme Court are important institutions to see that the government does not trespass on the rights of its citizens and works within the powers allocated to it by the Constitution. The judicial review enforces rule of law. Sathe (2002:5) points out that there can be two models of judicial review. One is a technocratic model in which judges act as technocrats and hold a law invalid if it is ultra vires the powers of the legislature. The other is a model, where the Court interprets the Constitution liberally in terms of rights and liberties of the citizens. In India, in recent years, the Court has furthered the rights of the disadvantaged sections and provided greater access to justice to them. This has raised considerable debate regarding the role of the Court and 'judicial activism'.

It is through 'judicial activism' that the Supreme Court has stepped on some controversial ground. As Sathe(2003:4) points out, " The Supreme Court started off as a technocratic court in the 1950s but slowly started acquiring power through constitutional interpretation." This interpretation came under greater public attention when it began to expand the rights of the people by changing the laws regarding *locus standi.*

This was done by allowing access to judicial process by entertaining letters opposing legal acts and by allowing social activist organizations or individuals to plead cases on behalf of the poor and the marginalized. This is commonly known as public interest litigation. This has changed the entire nature of the judicial process which now became more participatory and democratic. It is this opening of the Court that has sometimes brought it into conflict with the executive and the legislature but also raised its stature as a protector of democratic rights.

In assessing the role of judiciary, Mehta (2005) finds it a deeply paradoxical institution. On the one hand, the Supreme Court through the exercise of the power of judicial review has managed to place limits on the powers of the Parliament and the Executive. Through the use of public interest litigation, it has become an important instrument of governance. In the absence of parliamentary legislation, it has made laws, it has made public policy pronouncements; held executive agencies accountable and directly taken over the supervision of executive agencies. The first amendment came only a year after the adoption of the Constitution and instituted numerous minor changes. Many more amendments followed, at a rate of almost two amendments per year since 1950. Many matters that would be dealt with by ordinary statutes in most democracies must be dealt with by constitutional amendment in India due to the document's extraordinary details. Citizens look upon it as the highest custodian of constitutional values and their rights. On the other hand, the rest of the Court system does not work well and complaints of inefficiency, poor enforcement and corruption are frequently mentioned against it. There were 2.5 crore cases pending in the subordinate courts and around

37.1 lakh cases in the High Courts. In addition, there were around 40,000 cases pending in the Supreme Court.[9]

A close scrutiny of the present performance report made public by the Chief Justice of India on the status of the judicial system shows that the vacancy situation of judges in Courts is quite serious.[10] Out of the sanctioned strength of 792 judges in the 21 high courts across the country, the working strength was 586. This works to 26% vacancies to sanctioned strength in the high courts. The subordinate courts had a sanctioned strength of 15,399 judges but carried 20% vacancies. This means that every court in this country needs more judges and this is a necessary if not sufficient condition for improving judicial performance.

The three primary institutions of governance that make policy, implement it and interpret it and uphold the law and rights of citizens have come under severe strain in the recent years. The Constitution itself has undergone 93 amendments.[11] The federal system has been evolving into a more decentralized system with states under different political dispensation than the Centre demanding more autonomy than what was available till 1980. Most of the state demands have been in the area of financial and administrative relations. Reconsideration of policy of central grants, plan funds and

9. Statement of the Minister of State for Law and Justice, *Indian Express*, December 27, 2006
10. *Times of India*, Dec 1, 2007
11. The first amendment came only a year after the adoption of the Constitution and instituted numerous minor changes. In the decades of 1970-90 more than 55 amendments were enacted with only 23 in the earlier periods. Many more amendments followed. Many matters that would be dealt with by ordinary statutes in most democracies must be dealt with by constitutional amendment in India due to the document's extraordinary detail.

centrally sponsored schemes is a reflection of the acceptance of the validity of state claims. The liberal era has also seen the strengthening of state abilities to ask for international finance more directly. States are now competing for foreign investments and willing to accept the conditionalities being prescribed by the international donors (Rudolph and Rudolph, 2001). The central government has begun moving away from a command system to a more regulatory system.

The performance of constitutional institutions of governance has also become a cause of concern. There have been different explanations for the poor performance of these institutions. The issue is that the state has not been able to meet the aspirations of the people and the institutions are unable to meet the demands being made on them (Kohli, 1990). It is also contended that the institutions have been captured by certain social classes who have in turn subverted their goals to their own benefit (Bardhan, 1998). Others have laid the blame on the failure of policies that were followed and to a centralized planned economy (Bhagwati, 1995). Recently, there has been some attempt to relate the performance of the institutions to their institutional design and their adaptability to the changing circumstances (Kapur and Mehta, 2005). The assessment is not very easy but the fact remains that there is a rising dissatisfaction with the quality of governance.

Chapter III

Indian Bureaucracy and Administrative Reform

Indian administration continues to be in the mould of its colonial predecessor in spite of many efforts at reform. One single important characteristic of administrative system is its centralizing tendency and with the fact that All India services have been so conceived as to control administration from the central level to the district and local level. In the federal distribution of powers, most of the developmental subjects were assigned to the states and hence the responsibility of implementing policies related to them. But in the course of planned development, policies began to emanate from the Centre which also took upon the responsibility to see that these policies were implemented in a way that reflected central concerns. Central administration was expected to guide the state administration but soon transformed its own role and created a control and command system.

The determining factor in this transformation was the role of the Indian Administrative Service whose members were given key positions in the Centre and the States. They were Secretaries to government and in the parliamentary system the chief policy advisors of the ministers. All positions of District Collectors/Deputy Commissioners were also held by them.[12] The fact that members of the IAS held all critical

12. This is the general picture. There have been some Secretaries in recent years who are not from the IAS cadre but they are usually

positions in Government at all levels made them very influential. They provided leadership in all tasks to other cadres by their attitudes, values and style of functioning. Apart from the fact that the IAS considered itself as the successor of the Indian Civil Service of the pre-independence era, the primacy of the IAS in the system of governance in the country emanates from certain structural characteristics.

The recruitment to the IAS is done through a constitutionally established Union Public Service Commission and the induction training is provided by a central training institution. After confirmation in the service, a member of the IAS is allotted to a cadre of any one state but service conditions are determined by the rules and regulations established by the central government. His service, therefore, is so protected that in a case where he feels aggrieved by any action or non-action of the state government, he can appeal to the Centre. The purpose of such arrangement is to guarantee him independence and assure him immunity from local influences. But this network of control also makes him look up to the Centre for all career prospects. More often than not, this makes him more amenable to central directives. The Centre in turn finds him a useful conduit through which control over field activity can be exercised.

The IAS was moulded as a monolithic instrument and an image of elitism was deliberately built in to provide a sense of separation from the common society. This was supported by frequent movement of officials from one position to another and a few people, whirled about by rapid transfers, were

located in technical ministries. The dominance of the IAS has not been disturbed. District Collector has continued as the primary officer even when complex developmental organizations have multiplied at that level.

propelled by automatic promotions into higher positions exclusively reserved for them at all levels of government. On the way they commanded handsome salaries and social status forever denied to others (Potter, 1986).

Following the colonial structure of administration, the district collector continues to be the head of the district and all other government offices subservient to him. A direct line of command was established with centre/state authorities and the district officer was recognized as the kingpin of the system. The schemes of decentralization introduced after independence tended to strengthen rather than weaken this role. When the Community Development Programme was introduced, a parallel developmental hierarchy was created. The territorial divisions established for the purpose of collecting revenue were now supplemented by developmental divisions ensuring the reach of extension workers. The revenue hierarchy rose from the office of the Patwari, Tehsildar, Sub-Divisional Officer and reached up to that of the District Collector. The parallel development hierarchy began with a Village Level Worker, Block development Officer rising to that of the District Development Officer. Ironically the two positions of District Collector and District Development Officer were held by the same person belonging to the IAS. Vesting so much power in an individual meant that higher levels of government came to depend on him for all information and advice pertaining to his local area.

At the central level, there is a Secretariat servicing the elected political leaders. Each Ministry is headed by a Secretary and the top positions in every Ministry are usually occupied by the members of the IAS. The hierarchy is such that the initial years of service are spent by the members of the IAS in the districts and those who rise to become secretaries have only a few years to serve before retiring from service. In between, these IAS officers move from one position to another at the state and central level. The most coveted position continues to be that of the Secretary to the government ending into one position - that of Cabinet Secretary.

The striking characteristic of the Indian administration is the dominant role of the IAS in all decision-making in government. It holds all critical positions and works in tandem with political masters in implementing public policies. In numbers it is a small band of civil servants. There are around 400 IAS officers while the total number of central government employees is estimated to be around 42 lakhs in 1994. The large number of government employees hides the fact that the highest proportion of them consists of those who are non-decision-makers or part of what have come to be known as C and D categories of staff. These employees usually hold non-transferable jobs and have few chances of promotion.

The faith in ability of the state to be able to take up enormous tasks of development stemmed from the perceived strength and efficiency of the bureaucracy that the British colonial rulers had left behind. At a time when the other developing countries were struggling to establish a professional and career based civil service, the prestige and standing of the Indian Civil Service (ICS) was exceptional. It had served the colonial masters well and in the initial years of independence, provided tremendous support in quelling riots that followed partition of the country and in helping the integration of the country. The erstwhile masters had quickly taken over the role of upholding the law of the new sovereign state.

From the very beginning of the planning era, the task of implementing the development strategy was entrusted to the civil service, even though Nehru had demanded a radical transformation of the ICS during the independence movement, and it had been left to Patel to argue for its place in the Constitution. The ICS was seen to present state interests and to be relatively autonomous of local pulls and pressures. The doctrine of neutrality and impartiality was seen as its predominant behavioural trait, and it was assumed that its successor, moulded in the same tradition, would withstand the parochial pressures on the state. Together with Nehru, civil servants were the vanguard for the lobby for an industrial strategy, which created and expanded the public sector. However, the national orientation and professional ethos soon lost its gloss because public sector undertakings and other developmental projects could not be managed efficiently and effectively.

While the Indian bureaucracy is often cited as having Weberian characteristics, it is not known for creating sufficient state autonomy to pursue developmental interests. It has turned out to be weak instrument of the state and the network that it has created has usually been of rent making variety. There is increasing evidence that the alliance between the politicians and the bureaucrats has been in the pursuit of mutual gain. The demands of career advancement are of paramount significance for a civil servant and an obliging politician is willing to do anything for the civil servant who bends rules to favour his political master. The close linkage of civil servants with caste or communal groups, business houses and the large farmer community has to be seen as serving mutual interests (Bhambhri, 1998). In spite of this way of actual working, the civil service has grown up in the belief that it is the only group in the political system that works for public interests. It has not been easy for it to give up this self-perception and this has considerably weakened its ability to mobilize support for public policies and their implementation.

In this process, another significant development took place. Over the decades the bureaucrats emerged as powerful component of the decision-making process, largely because the political establishment was too happy to abdicate its responsibility to concentrate more on matters that were political. In providing continuity in civil administration despite political turbulence and change in governments, bureaucracy also proved to be an obstacle in the path of prompt action. "Redtapism" is as much a product of rulebook written by the government as its interpretation and application by bureaucrats. The show of the book has undoubtedly provided the crucial checks and balances required to prevent abuse of power by political authority. But it also led to another consequence. The show of the book as also the style of functioning of the new breed of politicians who see the rule book as an impediment and find the bureaucracy a needless obstacle that conflicts in relationships have emerged. The bureaucrats are apprehensive about their future and their career while the politicians are in a hurry to do things and create a future for themselves in their short tenures. Convergence of these interests has led to the formation of the kinds of alliance mentioned above.

The first serious assault on the nature of the civil service came from Mrs. Gandhi and other leaders of the Congress Party in 1969 in the form of demand of a 'committed' civil service. Long before independence, Nehru had expressed strong views about the Indian Civil Service (ICS) and how it had no place in modern India. But during his tenure as Prime Minister, members of the ICS became pillars of his economic and social policies and hence' during the initial years of planning, criticisms of bureaucracy for failing at development tasks were muted. But the situation changed drastically after Nehru's death in 1964. The Congress party, although remaining in power at the Centre, was considerably weakened and many states escaped its control. After the Congress split in 1969, issues of the bureaucracy's inability to implement socialist goals of the Party were brought to the top of the political agenda and the doctrine of neutrality was challenged. Mrs. Indira Gandhi was the Prime Minister[13] when, in his Presidential address in 1969, the President of the Congress Party called for a committed civil service by saying that "the so called neutral administrative machinery is a hindrance, not a help." He argued that "the present bureaucracy under the orthodox and conservative leadership of the ICS with its conservative upper class prejudices can hardly be expected to meet the requirements of social and economic change along socialist lines" (*Hindustan Times*, December 1969). Such a public statement by the organizational leader of the ruling party raised a national debate in which civil servants actively participated to defend themselves (see Dubhashi, 1971; Chaturvedi, 1971; *Seminar* 1973). The outcome was that the civil service gained a political image even though it insisted that it offered only professional advice.

The political role of civil servants was sharply delineated in the reports of the Shah Commission appointed by the Janata government to inquire into excesses of the 1975-1977

13. Writing to a friend in 1966 when she had just taken over as Prime Minister, Mrs. Gandhi said, "the intertia of our civil service is incredible" and added "we have a system of deadwood replacing deadwood." (quoted in Guha,2007:499)

Emergency imposed by Mrs Gandhi.[14] Some senior civil servants were clearly identified as owing allegiance to the Congress-I Party (read Mrs Gandhi) and were "harassed" or not given appropriate appointments when Mrs Gandhi lost the 1977 General Elections. The Shah Commission suggested that most IAS officers in secretariats and districts accepted orders they believed to be improper and politically motivated. There were many cases where officers "curried favour with politicians" by doing what they thought people in authority desired. An impact of such developments has been that Secretaries to government are often transferred or reshuffled when a new cabinet or even a new minister assumes power. The cabinet ministers demand civil servants on whose professional advice they can rely.

As Das (1998:148) says, by the time the Emergency (1975-77) ended, colonization of the civil service was complete. Even in the perception of the IAS officers themselves, the Service had changed irrevocably during the period. In a strong indictment, a retired civil servant says that bureaucrats have learned to adjust to the compulsions of politicians. In fact, the more enterprising among them have learned to anticipate the wishes of their political masters and to deliver unasked whatever is necessary for their personal and political welfare. Such bureaucrats earn a reputation and get ahead (Swarup 1990). A prominent civil servant writing in 1983 pointed out those newly elected ministers usually wanted to do certain things — "possibly in fulfilment of

14. Shah Commission of Inquiry appointed by Government of India in 1977 to enquire into all excesses committed during the Emergency (1975-77) imposed by Mrs. Gandhi. It was headed by Justice JC Shah , a retired Chief Justice of India.

electoral promises given generously rather than wisely. The civil servant in advising the minister has often to point out obstacles and pitfalls in pursuing that course of action even though in the end they must carry out the orders. Experienced and confident ministers welcome such advice. Less experienced ministers interpret such advice as obstruction. As the proportion of less experienced ministers increases, the more there is a ministerial preference for administrators who support their line of action without raising uncomfortable questions or doubts" (cited in Potter 1986:158).

From Professionalism to Loyalty

No formal change took place but the practice of shifting bureaucrats on demands of political leadership began a characteristic that is spread widely in the system today. Demand for loyal civil servants has spawned a transfer industry (Banik, 2001, Potter, 1986, Das,1998). Tenures of civil servants have become too short to hold them accountable for their performance. The number of IAS officers who have spent more than three years in their respective postings has been consistently less than 10% during 1978 to 1996. (Das, 1998) Mass transfer of officials becomes a routine every time there is a regime change. Such changes are more visible at the state levels but the Central government in Delhi has certainly not been immune to the practice. Transfers have become an important instrument of taming bureaucracy.

Transfers served several purposes in moulding the traditions in the British colonial service. Foremost, it was the most important method of creating a generalist civil service. Bright young men, with specialization in any subject from linguistics to botany to economics, were chosen through a competitive examination. What was judged was the quality of the intellect and not knowledge in a particular subject. Having had this assured through the recruitment process, the next step was to allow the civil servant to move from one post to another, while technical experts stayed put in subordinate departments or offices. The whole structure of the Raj celebrated generalist control and continuity, not specialist expertise and innovation (Potter, 1986:34). Often, transfers were too quick for the liking of individuals but were accepted for they were assumed to fulfill a particular purpose (Spangenburg, 1976).

Transfers also served two other purposes for the colonial administration. One was to avoid excessive 'embeddedness' in local society by creating some distance between the civil servants and local society (Banik, 2001:107). This was also meant to reduce the influence of caste, family relationships or friendships detrimental to the functional duties. The other purpose was to acquaint the British recruits to the diversity of life in India. British young men, who would be spending most of their working life in India, needed to be acquainted with its complexities of culture and difficulties of terrain.

The idea of a generalist civil service, beginning with the competitive examination in various subjects and interviews, was what provided continuity to Indian administration after independence. Transfers as a policy were part of this legacy and all that the Indian administration attempted was to fix a kind of a norm of a three year tenure in a single posting. This norm was rarely adhered to in practice. *The Indian Express* 30 May 2007, has reported in its headlines that Prime Minister Man Mohan Singh's government has started fixing 'minimum tenure' for officers of All India Services in the states. Under the new rules being framed, every officer would be assured continuity at a job for a tenure specified by the state, and any transfer –before the guaranteed period – can be done only on the recommendations of a Committee on Minimum Tenure.

However, it must be emphasized, all transfers are not a consequence of political choices to create a loyal team. Many transfers take place due to natural reasons like leave, retirements etc. A large number of transfers now take place due to the demand of the civil servants themselves. Some postings are perceived as difficult in terms of living conditions; others are considered not so lucrative. Some officers would like to live nearer home; others would like postings near the seats of power where their ambitions can be fulfilled. Thus, civil servants ingratiate themselves to political leadership for these favours. In return they are willing to be loyal and amenable to their demands. Those who have gained favours from one regime are then shunted out to give place to another group waiting in the wings.

Apart from the political initiative taken by Mrs. Gandhi to make the civil servants accountable for the implementation of development programmes, formal efforts to reform Indian administration have also been undertaken. The first significant report came from an American consultant Paul Appleby invited by the Finance Ministry in 1953. Only two of his recommendations viz. establishment of Indian Institute of Public Administration and of Organization and Methods divisions in the Ministries were accepted. Many more committees have been appointed.[15] A detailed review of the administrative system was provided by Administrative Reforms Commission appointed in 1966. This Commission

15. A list of committees and commissions appointed since independence for reforming Indian administration has been given by Maheshwari, (2004).

had a high powered chairperson in Morarji Desai who, however, resigned after a short while and was replaced by K Hanumanthaiya, a politician from Karnataka. This Commission set up 20 Study Teams, 13 Working Groups and one Task Force. It gave a total of 581 recommendations which were processed by the Estimates Committee of Parliament for approval. Some recommendations like a) the appointment of Lok Pal at the Centre and Lok Ayuktas in the states to deal with complaints of corruption and public grievances; b) constitution of Inter-State Council under Art. 263 of the Constitution for dealing with centre-state relations or c) the establishment of a central personnel agency Department of Personnel and Administrative Reforms were accepted.

But a major recommendation which, if implemented, would have meant a radical departure from the traditional character of the IAS, was not accepted. The ARC had suggested the regrouping of all the present civil services in the Government of India into eight functional categories, so that the IAS shall no more be a generalist civil service, but shall have a purely functional role of revenue administration (Jain, 2000:210). As a matter of fact none of the recommendations that would have changed the traditional core of its functioning were accepted and even the acceptance of recommendations regarding public grievance redressal system was half-hearted. Large amount of research involving equally large number of academics, civil servants and concerned citizens produced the recommendations for what needs to be done. Little headway was made, little impact on the lives of the common citizens took place even though the Estimates Committee dutifully reported to the Parliament on the number of recommendations that were accepted or were under consideration of the government.

The first reform effort, after neo-liberal economic reforms were introduced, was manifested in the Report of the Fifth Pay Commission in 1996. Recommendations for increasing the salaries of the civil servants were tied with recommendations for down-sizing the government. The scope of state activities was to be reduced and the size and number of government departments should reflect this. Large number of suggestions to prune and slim the government were made including that of outsourcing and partnerships with non-government organizations. However, what the government did was to accept recommendations regarding salary increases without accepting reduction in manpower. Currently, Second Administrative Reforms Commission, appointed in 2005 is at work.

The challenge of the task today has to be seen in the context of several features: a) little change has occurred from the kind of administration that we inherited from the colonial rulers b) in the process the administrative system has entrenched itself in a way that it has become more or less impervious to change c) powerful interests have developed in the status quo d) administrative reform has not been a high priority on the political agenda e) there has been failure at the conceptual level in generating alternatives. The present context of administrative reform is embedded in the assumptions of governance and liberal economic agenda. The state is being perceived as an enabling state that facilitates business and civil society to work together for development. Power orientation of administration has to give way to a perspective of partnership and cooperation with other actors of society. Far reaching transformation of civil services has to take place so that attitudes of domination can be replaced by those of democracy.

We must realize that high degree of bureaucratic autonomy and capacity may not necessarily lead to development because bureaucracy, as we have seen in Indian experience and elsewhere, has not been able to rise above its interests. On the other hand, market may not be the only answer for it cannot help those that are excluded from it because of various limitations. The solution lies in multiple institutions responding to the needs of the society. These can be bureaucratic, market or participatory institutions. What is needed for reform is the creation of a legal and constitutional situation where this multiplicity can grow. Participatory institutions or market institutions should not be stifled because of an overbearing law or because of lack of legal provisions. The more important direction that reform can take is in providing facilitative legal and contractual arrangements, explicit codification of rights as well as attendant obligations for new institutions to emerge and sustain themselves.

Annexure

List of Committees and Commissions on administrative reform established since Independence

1. The Reorganisation of Central Government (Richard Tottenham) 1945-46. (It visualizes an independent India; hence its inclusion here).
1. The Advisory Planning Board (K.C. Neogi), 1949.
2. The Secretariat Reorganisation Committee (Girija Shankar Bajpai), 1947.
3. The Central Pay Commission (Varadachariar).
4. The Economy Committee (Kasturbhai Lalbhai), 1948.
5. The Reorganisation of the Machinery of Government (Gopalaswami
6. Ayyangar), 1949.
7. Estimates Committee's Second Report on Reorganisation of the Secretariat and
8. Departments of the Government of India (First Lok Sabha), 1950-51.
9. Report on Public Administration (A.D. Gorwala), 1951.
10. Report on the Efficient Conduct of State Enterprises (Gorwala), 1951.
11. The Machinery of Government – Improvement of Efficiency (R.A. Gopalaswamy), 1952.
12. Public Administration in India – Report of a Survey (Paul H. Applyby), 1953.

Source: Maheshwari 2004

13. Estimates Committee's Ninth Report on Administrative, Financial and other
14. Reforms (First Lok Sabha), 1953-58.
15. Re-examination of India's Administrative System with special reference to administration of Government's Industrial and Commercial Enterprises (Appleby), 1956.
16. The Railway Corruption Enquiry Committee (J.B. Kripalani), 1955.
17. The Public Service (Qualification for Recruitment) Committee (A. Ramaswami Mudaliar), 1956.
18. The Commission of Enquiry on Emoluments and Conditions of Service of
19. Central Government Employees (Jagannath Das), 1959.
20. The Staff Welfare Review Committee (Fateh Singh), 1961.
21. Indian and State Administrative Services and Problems of District Administration (V.T. Krishnamachari), 1952.
22. The Committee on Prevention of Corruption (K. Santhanam), 1964.
23. Estimates Committee's Ninety-third Report on Public Services (Third Lok Sabha), 1966.
24. The Administrative Reforms Commission, 1966-70. It submitted the following nineteen reports.
    - i. Problems of Redress of Citizens' Grievances
    - ii. Machinery for Planning (Interim and Final)
    - iii. Public Undertakings
    - iv. Finance, Accounts and Audit
    - v. Economic Administration
    - vi. Machinery of Government of India and Procedures of Work
    - vii. Life Insurance Corporation
    - viii. Central Direct Taxes Administration
    - ix. Administration of Union Territories and NEFA
    - x. Personnel Administration
    - xi. Delegation of Financial and Administrative Powers

xii. Centre-State Relationships
xiii. State Administration
xiv. Small Scale Sector
xv. Railways
xvi. Treasuries
xvii. Reserve Bank of India

25. Posts and Telegraphs
26. Scientific Departments (only a summary of recommendations was submitted)

Besides the ARC set up the following 38 study teams :

i. Study Team on Machinery of the Government of India and its Procedures of Work
ii. Study Team on Economic Administration
iii. Study Team on Machinery for Planning
iv. Study Team on Centre-State Relationships
v. Study Team on Scientific Departments
vi. Study Team on Public Sector Undertakings
vii. Study Team on Financial Administration
viii. Study Team on Accounts and Audit
ix. Study Team on Promotion Policies, Conduct Rules, Discipline and Morale
x. Study Team on Recruitment, Selection, U.P.S.C / State Public Service Commissions and Training
xi. Study Team on Personnel Planning, Staffing of Public Sector Undertaking and Personnel Management
xii. Study Team on Redress of Citizens' Grievances
xiii. Study Team on District Administration
xiv. Study Team on Agricultural Administration
xv. Study Team on Administrative Tribunal
xvi. Study Team on State Level Administration
xvii. Study Team on Relations between the Press and the Administration
xviii. Study Team on Defence Matters

xix. Study Team on Railways
xx. Study Team on Union Territories Administration

Working Groups

i. Working Group on Police Administration
ii. Working Group on Railways
iii. Working Group on Medical and Health Administration
iv. Working Group on Cooperation
v. Working Group on Defence Production
vi. Working Group on Small Scale Sector
vii. Working Group on Central Direct Taxes Administration
viii. Working Group on Life Insurance Administration
ix. Working Group on Company Law Administration
x. Working Group on Posts and Telegraphs
xi. Working Group on Development, Control and Regulatory Organizations
xii. Working Group on Financial Rules
xiii. Working Group on Customs and Central Excise Administration

Expert Groups

i. Expert Group on Biological including Medical Services.
ii. Expert Group on Earth Services
iii. Expert Group on Natural Resources (Agriculture, Flora and Fauna).
iv. Expert Group on Engineering Sciences including Materials (Production and Utilization) Research

Task Forces

i. Expert Group Task Force on Treasuries
ii. The Third Central Pay Commission (Raghuvar Dayal), 1973
iii. The Committee on Recruitment and Selection (D.S. Kothari), 1978

iv. The National Police Commission (Dharam Vira), 1979
v. The Economic Administration Reform Commission (L.K. Jha), 1983

27. The Fourth Central Pay Commission (P.N. Singhal), 1986
28. The Commission on Centre-State Relations (R.S. Sarkaria), 1987
29. The Committee to Review the Scheme of the Civil Services Commission (Satish Chandra), 1989
30. The Central Fifth Pay Commission (Pandian), 1997

Chapter IV Corruption: Institutions of Accountability

The Planning Commission in its National Human Development Report (2002:122) points out that corruption is the most endemic and entrenched manifestation of poor governance in the Indian society, so much so that it has almost become an accepted reality and a way of life. Merely shrinking the economic role of the state by resorting to deregulation, liberalization and privatization is not necessarily the solution to addressing the problem. The Report further stresses that 'prevalent institutional arrangements have to be reviewed and changes made where those vested with power are also made accountable, their functioning made more transparent and subjected to social audit, with a view to minimise the discretionary decisions. The Approach Paper to the 11th Five Year Plan echoes the same views when it says that that all efforts to achieve rapid and inclusive growth will come to nought if corruption is not checked. It goes on to emphasise that 'much needs to be done by both the Centre and the States to reduce the discretionary powers of the government, ensure greater transparency and accountability, and create awareness among citizens.

There are three institutions that have been established to hold public agencies and officials accountable for their public actions. These are the Comptroller and Auditor General of India, Central Vigilance Commission and Central Bureau of Investigation. While Comptroller and Auditor

General is a constitutional body, the other two have been established by an Act of the Parliament.

Comptroller and Auditor General of India (CAG)

CAG is the guardian of the public purse and it is his duty to see that only authorised expenditure is made out of the Consolidated Fund of India. To perform this duty impartially and properly, the Constitution envisaged that the office is independent of any control of the Executive. This is ensured through the appointment procedures and other job conditions. In this way, the constitution has assured that his position is equivalent to that of a judge of the Supreme Court. The audit reports of the CAG are presented to the Parliament through the Public Accounts Committee. This Committee has 15 members from the Lok Sabha and 7members from the Rajya Sabha representing both the Treasury as well as the Opposition benches. This Committee scrutinizes the Appropriation Accounts of the Government of India and the Audit Report presented by the CAG. The purpose of this scrutiny is to satisfy itself a) that the money shown in the accounts as having been disbursed were legally available for and applicable to the service or purpose to which they have applied or charged; b) that the expenditure conforms to the authority which governs it and that c) every re-appropriation has been made in this behalf under the rules framed by competent authority.

Public Accounts Committee, in short, scrutinizes the Report of the CAG in detail and then submits its report to the Parliament so that irregularities noticed by it are discussed and effective steps taken.

CAG conducts two kinds of audits. One is known as Regularity Audit which verifies that expenditures have been made according to rules and authorization and the other is Performance Audit which lays significant emphasis on assessing the efficiency and effectiveness of expenditure with due regard to economy with which the entities run their programmes and activities. There are several issues involved in the ability of the CAG to hold government and public officials really accountable. One is procedural. The CAG can act only through the Public Accounts Committee of the Parliament. He cannot call officers for clarification or discussion. This is the job of the PAC. The auditors can, at best, include a paragraph in their report mentioning a delinquency. CAG also does not have any power to impose any sanction

This procedural aspect spills over to more substantive aspect. This is the lack of sensitivity of public officials to the comments of the audit reports and inability to raise issues based on audit objections for public debate. According to the Annual Report of the CAG for 2005-06 on its website[16], performance audits were conducted on 211 topics including nine exclusive ones. Findings of these audits were included in 19 Performance Audit Reports and other transaction Audit Reports placed in the Parliament/legislatures. Some of the more important performance audits conducted during the year were:

- Functioning of Employees State Insurance Corporation;
- Revenue generation by Doordarshan and All India Radio; Prasar Bharti;
- Pradhan Mantri Gram Sadak Yojana (PMGSY);
- Pradhan Mantri Gramodaya Yojana (PMGY);
- Sarva Shiksha Abhiyan;

16. http://cag.nic.in/Activity/2005-06/actrep_05_06.htm

- Import of Cooking Coal- Steel Authority of India Limited;
- Telecom business- GAIL (India) Limited;
- Wireless-in-Local Loop- Telecom service in Bharat Sanchar Nigam Limited;
- Disinvestment of Government share-holding in selected Public Sector Undertaking during 1993-2003;
- Development of land by Delhi Development Authority;
- Fund management of National Capital Region Planning Board;
- Employees Provident Fund Organisation;Assessment of Information System (AST) in the Income Tax department;
- Implementation of Acts and Rules relating to consumer protection.
- Integrated Child Development Scheme;
- Flood control measures in Bihar;
- National Slum Development Programme;
- Health System Development Project in Orissa;
- Impact of the reproductive child health programme in Uttar Pradesh; and
- Water management for irrigation in Haryana.

In the field of Regularity audit, CAG approved 12 Transaction Audit Reports on the accounts of the Union Government for placing before the Parliament and 60 Audit Reports on the accounts of state governments/Union Territories for placing before their legislature during 2005-06. The aggregate money value of the transaction audit findings in the Audit Reports calculated on the basis of the norms/ criteria determined by CAG was Rs.12,782 crore. It is imperative that the executive furnishes replies/response to the various forms of reports generated and issued in the process of audit culminating in CAG's Audit Reports to Parliament and state/UT legislatures with a view to ensuring that the opinion of the executive is taken into account before finalizing the audit findings. In respect of the Audit Reports of CAG, the Government of India has prescribed, on the recommendation of the Public Accounts Committee, that ministries/departments must furnish replies to the draft of the paragraphs, which are forwarded to the secretaries of the ministries/departments demi-officially, within six weeks. Yet, the ministries/departments did not furnish their response to 744 draft paragraphs issued to them out of a total of 1,641 included in the Audit Reports approved by CAG for presentation to Parliament. In respect of the state/UT Audit Reports, the governments did not furnish replies to 107 of the total 1,394 paragraphs approved for inclusion in the Audit Reports of the state/UTs.

An important dimension of accountability is that the government needs to take corrective action on the basis of deviations pointed out by the Audit Reports. This means that the accountability framework also envisages not only response of the government but also an account of the remedial measures undertaken. But the Action Taken Notes on 5,381 paragraphs and remedial measures for 11,771 paragraphs were still awaited from Union and state governments respectively.

There is another issue involved. Audit Reports usually document deviations that took place several years ago, possibly during that time either officials involved in irregular practices have changed or the government has taken remedial measures. Das (2005:136) has drawn attention to the comment of the Fifth Pay Commission which said: 'Audit should be as concurrent as possible. Scandals and scams are known even while they are being planned and executed. If audit draws attention to them forthwith in a well publicized manner, such scandals can be halted in mid-stride. Post-mortems are useful but can only be conducted while the patient is dead. It is better to cure the patient and try to keep him alive.'

The impact of the functioning of CAG on making the government accountable has been marginal. This has happened in spite of the constitutional mandate of the institution, its statutory independence from the executive and its diligence etc (Das, 2005). Part of the responsibility for this ineffective accountability framework has to be shouldered by the Parliament. As already mentioned, it finds little time for such matters and members do not take up the issues raised in audit reports for critically appraising the government.

In recent years, CAG has attempted to bring in leading citizens as members of an Audit Advisory Board to help him create greater publicity of the work he does and thus help in creating greater environment of accountability. The current membership of the Board 2006-07 is the following:

Ex-officio Chairman

Shri Vijayendra N. Kaul, Comptroller and Auditor General of India

Members

Shri N.R. Narayana Murthy, Chairman of the Board and Chief Mentor, Infosys Technologies Ltd.,

Shri Naresh Chandra, Former Cabinet Secretary and Ambassador to the USA

Shri T.S. Krishna Murthy, Former Chief Election Commissioner of India

Dr. R.A. Mashelkar, Director General, Council of Scientific& Industrial Research

Shri Pratyush Sinha, Central Vigilance Commissioner

Shri Deepak Nayyar, Member, Knowledge Commission

Shri Dharam Vir, Former Dy. Comptroller and Auditor General

Shri C.P. Jain, Former Chairman, NTPC Ltd.
Shri C.L. Kaw, Former Chairman, Railway Board
Vice Admiral (Retd.) Avnish Rai Tandon
Ms. Sunita Narain, Director, Centre for Science and Environment

Ex-officio Members

Shri T.N. Manoharan
President, The Institute of Chartered Accountants of India
Dy. Comptroller and Auditor General
Dy. Comptroller and Auditor General (Commercial)
Dy. Comptroller and Auditor General (Local Bodies & Accounts)

Ex-officio Secretary to the Board

Director General (Audit)

Central Vigilance Commission (CVC)

Central Vigilance Commission was appointed in 1964 on the recommendation of a Committee on Prevention of Corruption chaired by K Santhanam. It was envisaged to play an advisory role for it was assumed that anti-corruption functions were better performed in the organization itself. The CVC was given a statutory status after the enactment of a law passed by the Parliament in 2003. It is now a multi-member commission with a Chief Vigilance Commissioner and two Commissioners. CVC is conceived to be the apex vigilance institution, free of control from any executive authority, monitoring all vigilance activity under the Central Government and advising various authorities in Central Government organizations in planning, executing, reviewing and reforming their vigilance work. It does not, on its own, investigate the complaints that it receives; for that work is done by Vigilance Officers located in each organization. The CVC advises the organization on the action to be taken on the basis of the reports submitted by these Vigilance Officers. It is not mandatory on the government to accept this advice. The CVC can also refer a case to the Central Bureau of Investigation. This is also an agency independent of CVC and can work on its own steam. The result is that CVC is a purely advisory body depending on investigations conducted by either departments themselves whose officials have been complained against or an agency over which it has no control.

The reports of the Commission are submitted to the Parliament but rarely have they been taken up for discussion. The Annual Reports of the Commission itself bring out its ineffectiveness in preventing corruption in the country. The latest Annual Report for 2005-06 is illustrative in this regard.[17] The main issue that the Commission itself has highlighted, and which is vital to its effectives, is the fact its advice is not mandatory. When the government department/organization does not accept its advice, there is nothing that it can do. However, one needs to examine the functioning of CVC. During the year under reference, 9694 complaints were received by the Commission, out of which around 57% were filed without any action because they were anonymous or vague and unverifiable. Around 33% of complaints were classified not under its jurisdiction and sent to the departments concerned for their consideration. Thus only a little less than 7% of total complaints lodged were sent to the Vigilance Officers and CBI for investigation. Considering the extent of corruption recognized by society neither does the number of complaints nor the number actually referred for investigation match the response of the CVC. Clearly CVC does not figure as an important institution to fight corruption.

17. http://cvc.nic.in/ar2005.pdf

Even in such cases where the CVC asks for investigation, there are inordinate delays in filing reports by the Vigilance machinery of the government departments concerned. According to the Annual Report of 2005-06, the following data emerges:

Complaints Pending for Investigation and Reporting

Year	Up to one year	Between 1-3years	More than 3 years
2004	375	290	392
2005	336	207	145

Customs and Excise department is among those that have delayed reports. In addition, as many as 1747 cases were pending for over six months for implementation of the first stage advice of the Commission and 769 cases pending for over six months for implementation of the second stage advice of the Commission.

Central Bureau of Investigation

CVC also relies on the Central Bureau of Investigation (CBI) for investigation of corruption cases. The CBI traces its origin to the Special Police Establishment (SPE) which was set up in 1941 by the Government of India. The functions of the SPE then were to investigate cases of bribery and corruption in transactions with the War & Supply Department of India during World War II. Superintendence of the S.P.E. was vested with the War Department. Even after the end of the War, the need for a Central Government agency to investigate cases of bribery and corruption by Central Government employees was felt. The Delhi Special Police Establishment Act was therefore brought into force in 1946. This Act transferred the superintendence of the SPE to the Home Department and its functions were enlarged to cover all departments of the Govt. of India. The jurisdiction of the SPE extended to all the Union Territories and could be extended also to the States with the consent of the State Government concerned.

The DSPE acquired its popular current name, Central Bureau of Investigation (CBI), through a Home Ministry resolution of 1963. Initially the offences that were notified by the Central Government related only to corruption by Central Govt. servants. In due course, with the setting up of a large number of public sector undertakings, the employees of these undertakings were also brought under CBI purview. Similarly, with the nationalization of the banks in 1969, the Public Sector Banks and their employees also came within the ambit of the CBI. The CBI deals with many kinds of cases and those of financial probity are only one of them even though anti-corruption work is its core function

In public perception, CBI is seen as an instrument of political policy of the government of the day and not much faith is placed on its investigations. But the paradox is that not much faith is placed on other agencies either. So CBI is given responsibility when an impartial investigation is demanded and then government resorts to CBI that is far removed from the field of action and commands stature because it is a central agency. This usually happens when a case acquires political overtones due to lack of faith in local vigilance agencies. Das (2005) has documented some cases that took a political turn and did not yield any punitive results. Anti-corruption cases against senior government officers and political leaders are one of its more important functions. But its hands are tied in this regard because of another government ruling. All officers of the rank of joint secretary and above can be proceeded against only with the permission of the government. Cases against elective public officials can also be proceeded against with the permission of government. Sometimes this permission is difficult to come by; at others, investigation either gets distorted or proceeds at snail's pace risking disappearance or destruction of evidence.

It is clear from the above that the constitutional and statutory institutions established to check financial irregularities and fight corruption have not been effective. Institutions have been designed in a way that their reports meander through government corridors before being made public. CAG, to be effective, has to persuade the Public Accounts Committee of the seriousness of his findings. This Committee, in turn, has to attract Parliamentary attention to focus on what it considers the important lapses of the government. The process is time consuming, even the CAG Reports are based on events that happened years back, and public interest fades away. With little cognizance of the Reports from the Parliamentarians, officials see no reason to take them seriously and do not respond to the audit objections or remedial measures taken. The CVC is dependent on the government agencies, where the officials, against whom complaints are lodged, are located, for investigation. It has no control over the quality of investigation and time taken for reporting. If anti-corruption is taken as the major characteristic of good governance, India has to re-examine these institutional arrangements to make them more effective.

Chapter V

Governance and Decentralization

Decentralization has emerged as the key element in the present discourse of improving governance. It has become a very fashionable term and all countries, whatever their mode of government, are vying with each other in experimenting with decentralization (Manor, 1999). In its career, decentralization has assumed multiple meanings allowing each government to frame its own distinct policies. In India it has had a chequered history, beginning with the ideas of Gandhi for whom it was the cornerstone of alternative political and economic system that India should adopt when free and independent. The introduction of liberal economic reforms and the adoption of a new agenda for improving governance in the country from 1991 set decentralization in a different perspective. In between was the period of centralized planning where the concerns of decentralization were closely linked with achievements of plan targets.

While decentralization has been part of the Indian political lexicon from the time Gandhi framed his ideas about reconstructing Indian polity, it seems to have acquired a different perspective in the emerging discourse of governance. The contribution of governance perspective, in shifting the focus away from government, has been to recognise the inability of traditional political institutions to govern society through a top down approach. It was widely accepted that in a democracy, the political values and preferences of the government reflect the will of the people. The government translates this will of the people into laws and then implements it through its bureaucracy. The governance perspective directs attention to the role of multiplicity of actors and institutions in political decision-making and stresses that state, market and civil society were in a kind of network relationship in steering the society (Rhodes, 2000). Public policy is formulated and implemented through a plethora of formal and informal institutions, mechanisms and processes. The architecture of governance is a complex one and there are many centres of power and many actors and agencies that influence decision-making (Pierre, 2000).

Governance in a way decentred government and within its conceptualisation lies the notion of dispersal of power in society. At one level, there is considerable debate on the space that state, market and civil society occupy. The increasing reports about the failure of State directed economic development and failure of bureaucratic welfare state prompted the neo-liberals to push for 'less state and more market'. Market would help better allocation of resources and more efficient production and provision of public goods and services. Thus, in the context of neo-liberal economic policies governance came to mean reduction of the role of the state and increase in the roles of market and civil society. At another level, governance has meant recognition of spatial distribution of power and its multiple centres. These multiple centres can be at various spatial levels rising from the local community itself. Thus, the traditional political question raised issues about the capacity of state and its institutions in 'steering' society. Questions in governance are regarding issues concerned with society and the focus is on coordination and self-governance as such, manifested in different types of networks and partnerships (Rhodes, 1997).

In this perspective, the focus is on the capacity of society to govern itself. This capacity is related to its ability to make choices and articulate its preferences so that multifarious societal institutions including the state can translate them into action. But state is not the exclusive institution among the many institutions of market and civil society to take collective action. For this to happen, people must have institutional opportunities to participate in these processes. Thus, governing should be about what the public wants and finding ways of delivering those services (Peters, 2001:50). Participation and decentralization are key elements in the current discourse on democratic governance.

Current efforts at decentralization from the beginning of 1990s culminated at a time when discourse on governance together with that of economic liberalization was emerging as the dominant element of policy agenda. Decentralization was also seen as part of a wave of democratization that was sweeping many countries towards the end of 1980s (Blair, 2000:21). International donors were inspired to support numerous democratic local government programmes and by the end of 1990s USAID was supporting about 60 and UNDP more than 250 such activities around the world. Thus decentralization was on both national and international agenda.[18] But this also meant that decentralization acquired

18. The efforts at decentralization were not donor driven though. The World Bank and the IMF tended to lag behind governments in less developed countries. However, some donor countries began to shift their emphasis away from large scale development programmes to more modest, micro-level projects into which grassroots communities could be drawn in as participants, in the hope of making development more sustainable. (see Manor 1999:29).

different meanings for different people. To the liberal economist decentralization is a way of getting rid of the interventionist and over extended or predatory state. In the literature on structural adjustment and transitional reform, decentralization is sometimes used as a synonym for privatization (Bardhan 1996:140). In the governance discourse, it means dispersion of power at the local level and control by self-governing communities. In India, then, decentralization began to mean dispersion of power not only to rural and urban self-government but also to self-help groups, local communities and NGO's. The three five year plans – Eighth, Ninth and Tenth have provided broadest meaning to decentralization and have not just confined themselves to panchayat raj or municipal government.

There is another point that needs to be noted. The efforts in the 1990s were in no way a response to any pressure building on the ruling elites from people below. They were a response to the demands of elites at the state level and opposition parties lobbying for greater devolution. This is not to deny that a social and political awakening had been occurring over the last three decades that persuaded central leaders to consider decentralization as a method to cope with the new social forces. Rajiv Gandhi was concerned with devolution for developmental reasons and therefore the amendment that was introduced by his government was limited in its financial and administrative scope even though guaranteeing periodic elections but the Act that was finally passed aimed at creating local self governing institutions. It is only now in 2003 that some popular moves for more effective decentralization are emerging. Recently Federation of Empowerment of Local Governments and Lok Satta launched a campaign to collect 'one crore' signatures in support of local government empowerment in Andhra Pradesh. Campaign begun on 9th August 2003 ended on 2nd October with more than the target achieved. It was not only an effort to place demands on Andhra Pradesh government but to widen awareness about the importance of empowerment and to show that it was not an issue within the domain of politicians alone.

Constitutionalizing Local Governance

Second generation panchayats in West Bengal, Karnataka and Andhra Pradesh had evoked considerable enthusiasm during the 1980s because they were created more as political rather than as purely developmental entity. Rajiv Gandhi government modelled a Bill on the lines that LM Singhvi formulated as an appendix to the Ashok Mehta Committee Report. In 1989, when the 64th Amendment to the Constitution was introduced it was defeated because of lack of support in the Rajya Sabha. Opposition to the Amendment emanated from the states which felt the Centre was intervening directly with local level and also attempting to introduce uniformity in the country (Mathew 2000:9). It was left to Narsimha Rao government to introduce the 73rd and 74th Amendments to the Constitution in 1992 and have them enacted in 1993 after such opposition had been overcome. Panchayats and urban governments had now constitutional support.

These amendments were a move towards creation of local self-government institutions but fell short of this expectation because of the way powers and responsibilities were endowed on them. The Amendment left devolution of powers on the discretion of the state legislature when it said that '....(it) may by law endow the Panchayats with such powers and authority as may be necessary to enable to function as institutions of local self-government..' and with respect to 'a) the preparation of plans of economic development and social justice; b) the implementation of schemes for economic development and social justice as may be entrusted to them including those in relation to matters listed in the Eleventh Schedule.' (For subjects listed in the 11th Schedule see Annexure to the chapter) In its provisions, the Act was not mandatory and allowed some states to delay implementation or respond inadequately. The scope of responsibilities particularly those concerned with law and order were excluded and subjects in the Eleventh Schedule were only suggestive.[19] The result is that while the Constitution envisages considerable autonomy to these institutions, states have been reluctant to part with their powers. Except Kerala, there has been little attempt in other states to use the Amendment to develop institutions of self-government for local governance (for elaboration see the discussion in Bandopadhyaya et.al. 2003).

However, the Constitutional Amendment Act made several significant advances over the past. It made it mandatory that elections will be held every five years and will be conducted by State Election Commission. A uniform three tier structure was envisaged with Gram Sabha or the village assembly as the deliberative body of decentralised governance and as the foundation of the panchayat system. Women empowerment was mandated by reserving one-third

---

19. In his dissenting note to the Asoka Mehta Committee Report, EMS Namboodiripad had argued that "I cannot think of Panchayati Raj Institutions as anything other than an integral part of the country's administration with no difference between what are called the 'development' and 'regulatory' functions." (see Government of India 1978:163).

seats in all the elected bodies as well as among the office of chairpersons in each tier. Reservations for scheduled castes and tribes were also provided. To ensure adequate financial resources to the panchayats, the Act has envisaged setting up a State Finance Commission every five years. District Planning Committees were made mandatory and given constitutional status.

A virtual democratic revolution has been brought about with 30 lakh representatives getting elected at the local level every five years out of whom 10 lakh are women. Women are also occupying positions as head of panchayats. But states like Bihar held elections after a delay of 23 years and Assam after that of nine years. In few states like Andhra Pradesh, Gujarat and Punjab elections for all the tiers were not held at a time.

The Constitution in its Article 243G mandated that the legislatures of a State may, by law endow the Panchayats with such powers and authority as may be necessary to enable them to function as *institutions of self-governance* (italics mine). It further listed 29 subjects in the 11th Schedule with reference to which powers and functions could be devolved to the Panchayats. The intention of the Amendment was that these institutions would be able to act autonomously within the domain delegated to them by the State laws. Nothing of this sort happened. The conformity legislations of most States have not significantly altered the functional domains of the gram panchayats across the country. A study of 15 states showed that in cases of higher levels of Panchayats, previous provisions were repeated wherever earlier Acts existed and also no additional grant of powers, administrative staff was done to enable them implement whatever responsibilities given (Fernandes 2003:2874). On the other hand, funds or staff is retained by the line departments of state governments which continue to function, as before, independently of Panchayats even in respect of subjects which are supposed to be within the domain of the panchayats (Panchayati Raj Update, December 2001).

Autonomy to act within the domain has been further constrained by continued existence of administrative departments at the district level and below whose activities have continued as if the constitutional obligations to create local self-governing institutions do not exist. The District Rural Development Agencies, that have been the traditional institutions, at the district level to implement and oversee implementation of anti-poverty schemes have not been wound up and according to the Mid-Term Review and Appraisal Report (Government of India 2006:129) around 571 of the them are working in the country. Besides, new institutions set up by the government in partnership with civil society like in the field of joint forest management or watershed development have introduced further complexity. None of these agencies are accountable to the Panchayats even though their functional domains overlap. The complexity of the local web of institutions increases with the non-government organizations coming in to support large number of self-help groups and community based organizations that work for specific aspects of rural development.

What is paradoxical is that while Panchayats suffer from paucity of funds the other local agencies do not. In 1993, the Prime Minister announced a Local Area Development Scheme (LADS) within which the MPs could direct the

District Collectors to take up projects of Rs. 1 crore in their constituency.[20] Twenty-three schemes like constructing school buildings, village roads, hospitals or sports/cultural activities can be supported under this scheme. Interestingly, all the 23 items of work meant to be implemented by the MPs fall in the subjects allotted in the 11th schedule. MPs use the scheme to earn patronage. The effort to develop a plan and respond to the priorities based on local aspirations becomes difficult because the MPs use their schemes for political rewards. Many states have also provided some funds to their MLAs on the same pattern. Several municipalities have also started similar scheme for their Councillors (for example, Rajasthan and Delhi). This is a dangerous portend and a deplorable inroad into the domain of the local bodies (Mathew 2000:18). It has been appropriately called an assault on the Constitution by another observer(Venkataramaiah 1997; see also PRIA 2000).

In addition, large amount of funds are earmarked for centrally sponsored schemes implemented at the local level. The Standing Committee of the Thirteenth Lok Sabha on Urban and Rural Development points out in its 37th Report (2002) more than Rs. 40,000 crore of the total plan outlay under the Centrally Sponsored/Central Sector schemes and about Rs. 31,000 crore of annual outlay of the State plans, partly or wholly related to 29 subjects mentioned in the Eleventh Schedule are implemented by the State governments at the state and district levels. It goes on to suggest that the proportion of scheme funds implemented at the District level should be transferred to the PRIs proportionately according to their needs. The Committee has repeatedly recommended

20. Today the amount under the MPLADS is Rs. 2 crore and each project can cost upto Rs.10 lakhs.

that all centrally sponsored schemes should be transferred to the Panchayats (Government of India 2006).

Another aspect of the creation of self-governing institutions was the establishment of District Planning Committees. According to Article 243 ZD 'there shall be constituted in every state at the district level a District Planning Committee to consolidate the plans prepared by the Panchayats and the municipalities in the district and to prepare a draft developmental plan for the district as a whole.' Most states like Assam, Bihar Gujarat, Himachal Pradesh, Maharashtra and Punjab, have not constituted such committees (see Appendix 2).

Lack of financial devolution is another serious impediment in furthering the intentions of the Amendments. Panchayats are to a great extent dependent on the states for grants. Even though First State Finance Commissions were constituted by all the states, acceptance of their recommendations has been uneven. Kerala, Madhya Pradesh, Punjab, Rajasthan, Tamil Nadu, Uttar Pradesh and West Bengal are among the states, which have accepted the Report in full. However, none of the states have disbursed funds according to the recommendations (Panchayati Raj Update July 2000). Even with this disappointing background (Mathew 2000), the Eleventh Finance Commission sanctioned Rs.1600 crores annually for Panchayats and Rs.400 crores for municipalities to be distributed among the states.

It is clear that states are reluctant to share their powers and resources with the panchayats. States have not realised that the Amendments have created qualitatively different kind of institutions of local governance, which curtails state bureaucratic functions at the local level and replaces them by a democratic set of institutions. In passing the conformity

Acts, it is precisely this that the States have been careful not to do. Local governments are dependent on the state governments and are 'nothing more than their agency' (Bandopadhyay et.al. 2003:3989). Only Kerala is an exception. It is reported that the Centre would move another constitutional amendment making it mandatory for state governments to transfer at least 11 of the 29 powers in the 11th Schedule with 'funds and functionaries' (The Hindu 2003). This appears to have come after the plea of the Prime Minister himself that 'in the Amendments Panchayats have been visualised as the 3rd tier of governance in the federal polity' (Panchayati Raj Update June 2001). But the hope of the Prime Minister cannot be realized when some states are launching their own institutions of local governance. Andhra Pradesh has launched a Janmabhoomi programme that is receiving large amount of funds from the state government's sectoral programmes like those of rural employment or water supply etc. Madhya Pradesh has created a parallel district government structure making the District Collector quite powerful.[21]

In the aftermath of the amendments, the Kerala experience has been a unique one. The decentralization process through people's mobilization sought not only to devolve power from the state to the local level but also to elicit people's participation in the process of development. The objective of the People's Campaign for Decentralized Planning is not simply to draw up a plan from below. It was expected to bring about a transformation in the attitudes of the participants themselves (Isaac 2001:15). The People's

21. It is reported that the new government installed in Madhya Pradesh on Dec. 8, 2003 is proposing to abolish District governments.(see *Asian Age*, Dec.13, 2003 p.1)

Campaign has been described in detail (see in particular Isaac and Franke 2001). In its first phase, the effort was to create basic awareness and preparation for attending gram sabha meetings. It is estimated that more than two million persons participated in gram sabhas and ward committees. This generated public debate on development all over Kerala (Sharma 2003:3836). In the second phase of the Campaign development seminars were organized in every gram panchayat and effort to draw up development plans. Emphasis was laid on data collection and resource mapping. The third phase was concerned with projectization of development plans. This was the more difficult part of the campaign when resource persons had to be recruited and training programmes begun. Preparation of annual plans followed with the state governments issuing guidelines about sectoral allocation of funds.

Undoubtedly the Kerala experience gave new meaning to the exercise of decentralization in the country. It also showed how voluntary agencies like KSSP and others were significant in making the Campaign a success. The Kerala experience also highlights the critical role of the state government in activating the Panchayats.[22] It demonstrated that decentralization is more than rules and laws but a different culture of development requiring intense people's mobilization. Kerala experience signifies the diversity in implementing public policies towards decentralization in India.

The concept of self-governing institutions can be translated successfully on the ground only if the poor and the marginalized citizens are also able to participate in decision-

22. Several other lessons have been drawn by Sharma (2003) from the Kerala experience and also by Isaac and Franke (2001).

making. The Amendments recognise the disadvantaged position of those citizens who have been excluded from decision-making processes due to social, economic or gender criterion and therefore have provided reservation of seats at all levels of Panchayats in proportion to their share in population and reservation to offices of chairpersons of these institution. This provision brings the disadvantaged into the institutional set up for without it they may not have found representation but it does not necessarily ensure their actual participation in decision-making. One needs to explore the factors influencing actual participation. As suggested earlier, there is diversity of local experience in the country with the states responding differently to the freedom given to them in Amendments to the Constitution. Social and political contexts also differ.

Women Participation in Panchayats

The most important dimension of this widening democratic base has been the reservation of seats for women and dalits. It is not as if women have not participated in panchayats earlier. As far back as 1963-68, there was an all women Panchayat in Nimbut village in Pune district of Maharashtra. What is significant now is that women participation is mandated for all Panchayats through out the country. It has been estimated that of the total 26 lakh elected Panchayats representatives around 42% are women. However, this formal position has not necessarily led to substantive participation. Reservation resolves some of the problems but the constraints which stem from traditional village institutions and familial and socio-cultural forces still remain. Protagonists of reservation argue that the male dominated political system has so far refused to provide space to women and that reservations can create the space to enable the women to exert pressure on the system to bring their issues on the political agenda (Sharma 1998:36). There is evidence to show that in many areas that women attempt to address the more vital needs of women. As such, they work on schemes for bringing piped water into the village; inspect development works and nutrition centres under the ICDS; and pay particular attention to children's education. They also take the initiative in a variety of family and matrimonial matters, from abusive or alcoholic husbands to settling land disputes (CWDS, 1999:137 quoted in UNDP, 2003). There are many cases of individual Pradhans or Sarpanch who have done commendable work despite heavy odds. (See various issues of Panchayati Raj Update from 1997 onwards) In West Bengal, Kamala Mahato, a panchayat pradhan in Purulia district stands out as one who is commended for digging 10 wells for drinking water as well as for irrigation and initiating employment schemes under the IRDP programme. Similarly, the story of Fatimabee, a sarpanch of a village in Andhra Pradesh, caught the national imagination. She wore the traditional burqa and was illiterate but managed to get many things done for her village. Women members of a gram panchayat in Akola district of Maharashtra fed up with the drinking habits of their husbands and the atrocities following the drinking sessions were successful in closing the liquor shop doing brisk business in their village for the last twenty years.

However, such success stories are few and far between. They are overwhelmed with stories of exclusion and the way this is brought about. Social constraints feature a) patriarchal ordering of society that leads to tokenism and surrogate representation; b) illiteracy which deprives women participation in decision making; and c) low caste position combines the oppression of caste and patriarchy. One of the most extreme forms that social constraints take is the physical violence to which women and lower caste representatives alike have been subjected. This coercive mechanism of exclusion is more serious than simple disfranchisement that issues from illiteracy or patriarchal values that are enforced or internalised (UNDP, 2003:42).

Thus, despite the reservation women participation is a long struggle. Legislative Acts have given women avenues of empowerment but social constraints appear as serious obstacles. In Tamil Nadu, The Tamil Nadu Federation of Women Presidents of Panchayat Government and Tamil Nadu Federation of Dalit Presidents of Panchayat Government have been fighting for their rights. It is reported that the government accepted their plea not to rotate the posts reserved for Dalits and women allowing large number who served one term to get elected (Panchayati Raj Update February 2002:4). In the past few years, many more networks of elected women representatives have been created; the most notable experiments in networking and association formation have taken place in Karnataka, Gujarat and Kerala. Many non-governmental organizations support their activities[23] (Behar and Aiyar 2003).

Dalits in Panchayats

In spite of the statutes, Dalits face severe challenges in even getting representation. Santha (2002:1953) recounts the

23. The ground experience of the working of Panchayats strongly highlighted the continued need for effective capacity building. These associations are experimenting with various methods to strengthen the capacities of women representatives (Behar and Aiyar, 2003).

events in four gram panchayats in two districts of Tamil Nadu where Dalits were denied the democratic right to contest elections even for the reserved seats. This has been going on from 1996 and is happening in spite of the State Election Commission scheduling elections more than a dozen times since then and instructions from the National Commission for SCs/STs. In contrast, in Bihar, following a Patna High Court order, against which an appeal has been lying in the Supreme Court since 1996, reservation was withdrawn from all single posts in the Panchayat elections held in April 2002, as many as 124 Dalit candidates have registered their presence as Mukhias (Panchayati Raj Update October 2002:1952).

Once having elected, participation in meetings etc becomes important. In an empirical study conducted by Narayana (2005), findings are revealing. The study was conducted in one district and one block each of Madhya Pradesh, Tamil Nadu and Kerala. The participation of Dalits was as good as others in the Gram Sabhas. The most significant finding is that the participation of the poor in Kerala is higher than in other two states. These findings are corroborated in many ways in different states. In their study in West Bengal, Ghatak and Ghatak (2002) mention that the average attendance in Gram Sansad was low at 12% (10% is the quorum). They highlight the fact that generally participation level is low for all categories and so also of those of the disadvantaged category. Similar findings emerge from studies conducted in Madhya Pradesh (Beher, 2003) and Karnataka (Deshpande and Murthy 2002).

A number of explanations have been offered for this weak participation. Mathew and Mathew (2003:48) have argued that this is mainly because of lack of awareness and the feeling among the disadvantaged groups that their views are not taken seriously and their voices are not heard if the leadership is from dominant castes. Deshpande and Murthy (2002) have also argued that the long term solution lies in increasing the levels of awareness while Beher (2003) suggests that participation is higher in areas where there is greater activity of the NGOs.

A more popular and widely held explanation is that these problems are embedded in the wider socio-economic and political context in which the dalits are placed. The issue of participation is related to the radical transformation of society and the socio-economic upliftment of these groups. Asok Mehta Committee Report (1978:91) had argued that developments, which are likely to take place in the socio-economic structure of the country during the next decade, will determine the future role of the Panchayati Raj Institutions especially with reference to the weaker sections. At the local level the particular reference has been the inability to undertake land reforms to weaken the hold of the dominant castes. Undoubtedly structures of social and economic oppression have to be dismantled before the dalits can benefit from opportunities provided by the reservations and access to local institutions.

To complicate matters, institutions of local governance are not confined to the formal panchayat system. Informal institutions based on caste continue in most parts of the country. In a study done in three districts of Karnataka, Ananthpur (2004) provides data to show that apart from enforcing social rules and norms, these caste panchayats also perform range of functions like arbitrating disputes and carrying out some social functions. In many cases instead of building inter-caste solidarity, these panchayats uphold and coerce the disadvantaged to accept social norms that are detrimental to their interests and an instrument of keeping them under the domination of the upper castes. Newspaper reports highlight the stories of cruelty and violence meted out to the Dalits by these panchayats. As evidence from Rajasthan and Madhya Pradesh (Krishna 2002), Karnataka (Ananthpur, 2004) and West Bengal (Gupta, 2001) shows, these Panchayats are surviving in many parts of the country. The activities of these Panchayats in enforcing social norms will influence the way the Dalits choose to participate in formal Panchayats.

The major question is of empowering Dalits when the external environment is not necessarily favourable to them if not actively against them. Amendments to the Constitution and reservations in the local Panchayats were major actions that led to expansion of opportunities in participating in decision-making. However, participation as elected representatives has to be a source of empowerment in influencing development projects and mobilizing resources. Here is the major challenge. Available evidence indicates that the enhanced numerical presence in panchayat institutions of women and dalits has not generally meant that policies in their favour have been enunciated or implemented. Apart from the social factors cited above, the Panchayati Raj institutions suffer from paucity of resources. There are too little finances available at the gram panchayat level. For the first time the Eleventh Central Finance Commission, in its mandate, was asked to make recommendations to augment the resources of the Panchayats. It did so but also went on to express its concerns about the lack of commitment of Centre and States into making Panchayats 'institutions of self government.' It also expressed its serious concern that the states are not giving attention to the pivotal role of the State

Finance Commissions in strengthening the panchayats. The Commission has given a number of recommendations ranging from devolution of financial resources to those that are related to the strengthening of district plan committees. But the Commission's recommendation to give grant to the Panchayats of Rs. 8000 crores during 2000-05 will come as a considerable relief to them for maintaining civic services. Of this amount Rs.200 crores have been earmarked for development of data base on the finances of panchayats and municipalities and Rs.98.61 crores have been earmarked for maintenance of the accounts of the Panchayats. The civic services categorized by the Commission are drinking water, roads, culverts, bridges, ferries, waterways and other means of communication, rural electrification, health and sanitation including hospitals, primary health centers and dispensaries and maintenance of community. This is a meager amount considering the fact that the Commission itself quoted a NIRD study which estimated financial requirements for these services at Rs.1, 42,128 crores for a period of five years (Mahi Pal, 2000:4380). The result is that resources available for social welfare programmes are spread very thinly and rarely make an impact of significance.

What needs to be added is that the devolution of funds by the Eleventh Finance Commission to the local institutions has to be seen together with the recommendations of the State Finance Commissions. The revenue share for local bodies recommended by some of the SFCs is as low as 2.18% of the total net tax revenue of the state as in Rajasthan while in Karnataka it is 36% of the total non-loan gross revenue receipts. The State Finance Commissions have a responsibility to recommend measures to build up the financial capability at the local level. Otherwise fiscal autonomy cannot be promoted. On the contrary, if the local governments are allowed unrestricted transfers without an appropriate system of checks and balances fiscal profligacy can emerge. (Rani, 1999) The Standing Committee of the Thirteenth Lok Sabha on Urban Rural Local Government (2002) has suggested that the Union Government in consultation with State governments should carefully review and monitor on an on-going basis the recommendations of the 10th and 11th Finance Commissions for the 12th Finance Commission to take appropriate action.

In addition, many of the social welfare measures that are critical to the empowerment of Dalits are subject to centralized provision. Representatives of the Panchayats have very little influence on the way health and educational services are delivered. When primary health centers and primary schools fail, the worst sufferers are the poor and the marginalized.

Annexure

List of Subjects Which State Legislature Can Delegate to the Panchayats

ELEVENTH SCHEDULE
(Article 243G)

1. Agriculture, including agricultural extension.
2. Land improvement, implementation of land reforms, land consolidation and soil conservation.
3 Minor irrigation, water management and watershed development.
4. Animal husbandry, dairying and poultry.
5. Fisheries.
6. Social forestry and farm forestry.
7. Minor forest produce.
8. Small scale industries, including food processing industries.
9. Khadi, village and cottage industries.
10. Rural housing.
11. Drinking water.
12. Fuel and fodder.
13. Roads, culverts, bridges, ferries, waterways and other means of communication.
14. Rural electrification, including distribution of electricity.
15. Non-conventional energy sources.
16. Poverty alleviation programme.
17. Education, including primary and secondary schools.
18. Technical training and vocational education.
19. Adult and non-formal education.
20. Libraries.
21. Cultural activities.

22. Markets and fairs.
23. Health and sanitation, including hospitals, primary health centres and dispensaries.
24. Family welfare.
25. Women and child development.
26. Social welfare, including welfare of the handicapped and mentally retarded.
27. Welfare of the weaker sections, and in particular, of the Scheduled Castes and the Scheduled Tribes.
28. Public distribution system.
29. Maintenance of community assets.

Chapter VI

Network Governance for Economic Growth

As pointed out in first chapter, governance is concerned with network of relationships of three actors – state, market and civil society. It is an interactive process where government may like to impose its will but its acceptance will depend on compliance and action of others. One institution depends on another and this is what Stoker refers to as power dependence. In this relationships and networks, no one institution can easily dominate; it will depend on particular process of exchange. The monopoly of political institutions in providing services is diluted; the private sector and institutions of civil society fill in the space previously occupied by these institutions. New forms of institutions emerge and this finds expression in the blurring of boundaries between the public and the private sector. A range of voluntary agencies arise that respond to collective concerns.

The result is that the relationship between the government in India and the industrial corporate sector changed. During the Nehruvian era, rational allocation of resources, industrialization and modernization were the key words in the vocabulary of development and the thinking was that the state had the principal role in initiating development with the market functioning under its overall direction.

The Nehruvian perspective of modernization through

industrialization found support among industrialists, civil servants and intellectuals in pre-independence India. A concrete outline for an economic policy with this vision came from leading industrialists like Sir Purshottamdas Thakurdas, JRD Tata, GD Birla, Sir Shri Ram and Kusturbhai Lalbhai from Bombay. Popularly known as the Bombay Plan, their 'Plan for Economic Development for India' envisaged India's progress through the expansion of textile and consumer industries and viewed the role of state as that of providing investment in infrastructure and in industries where the private investment would not go (Thakurdas 1944). A slightly more technocratic support came from civil servants who were working in the princely states. Sir Ardeshir Dalal headed the Planning and Development Department set up by the colonial government after the Second World War. Sir M. Visvesvarayya, Dewan of Mysore as well as an engineer who had built reservoir dams and railway lines, insisted that 'industries and trade do not grow of themselves, but have to be willed, planned and systematically developed'. He pleaded for entrusting the task of planning for industrialization to a central intellectual 'brain' – an economic council of expert economists and businessmen – that would coordinate and direct policy for the whole of Indian society (Khilnani 1997:71). Consequently, the discourse on development was formulated in the technical vocabulary of economics, science and technology.

Thus, in Nehru's time, State was perceived as a rational state not tainted by day to day political pressures in its economic decision-making. Planning Commission was created and the Cabinet Resolution that laid down procedures for its functioning specified that it would make recommendations to the Cabinet and, in framing its recommendations, it will

- act in close understanding and consultation with the Ministries of Central Government and the Governments of the States. The responsibility of taking and implementing decisions will be that of the Central and State governments.

Thus, officially, the Planning Commission was envisaged as an advisory body allowing its technical proposals to be vetted by the political leadership of the government. Ultimately, the decisions based on its advice were therefore political decisions. However, Nehru envisioned a much greater role for the Planning Commission than merely giving advice. He set great store by the technocratic nature of this advice and went about giving the Planning Commission such status and prestige that would make it difficult for political leadership at the helm of ministries to ignore it. While Nehru lived, he chaired the Planning Commission, combining in himself the roles of chief advisor and chief implementer of the advice.

A consequence of the strategy of making the Planning Commission the main repository of technical advice was a perceptible rise in the power and influence of those who worked within the government. The urge of the government to seek advice from outside was considerably muted because there was a growing feeling that the best sources of advice were available within the government itself. Moreover, framing policy was regarded to be a technical matter. Hence, democratic participation of different groups in a society was not given much significance.

Foundation of a belief in a rational - technocratic state and its primacy in steering development was laid at this time (Chatterjee, 1998). Planning Commission's work relied on being insulated from wider deliberation about India's future and faith in the ability of the professionals and technocrats to do the best for it (Khilnani,1998). This has left a lasting perception on the Indian mind and every problem whether political or social is sought be solved through a committee of experts.

Another significant feature of the planned strategy for development was the faith in the ability of administration to implement the plans prepared by the technocrats and experts. From the very beginning of the planning era, the task of implementing the development strategy was entrusted to the civil service, even though Nehru had demanded a radical transformation of the Indian Civil Service (ICS) during the independence movement, and it had been left to Patel to argue for its place in the Constitution. The ICS was seen to present state interests and to be relatively autonomous of local pulls and pressures. The doctrine of neutrality and impartiality was seen as its predominant behavioural trait, and it was assumed that its successor the IAS, moulded in the same tradition, would withstand the parochial pressures on the state. Together with Nehru, civil servants were the vanguard for the lobby for an industrial strategy, which created and expanded the public sector (Rudolph and Rudolph, 1987). Leading advisers of Nehru, for example, were civil servants of the ICS variety: Boothlingam in finance and steel; CD Deshmukh, Vishnu Sahay and Tarlok Singh in planning; HVR Iyengar in commerce and industry and Reserve Bank of India; SS Khera in steel and mines and KB Lal in trade (Mathur, 1991).

It must also be noted that during the same period that the bureaucracy was being relied upon to implement the industrial licensing policy, the government was not closing the doors of consultation and advice from the private sector. The Industries Development and Regulation Act 1951 provided for a Central Advisory Council which was established to provide the representatives of business a forum to voice their views. Such advisory bodies, known as Development Councils, were established for individual ministries too.[24] Despite the government's thinking that consultation with the private sector was important in pursuing development policies and also the repeated amendments to the Act between 1951 and 1983 did not touch the provisions of the Council, the ministers and the bureaucrats found it too cumbersome to consult it particularly in areas where they thought that the government had pre-eminent role. The meetings, whenever held, turned out to be opportunities for business representatives to make long statements of demands and for government to exhort industry to work for public good. (Marathe 1989:63-90) Even this consultative arrangement with private sector declined significantly with the advent of Indira Gandhi in the late 1960s when the big business began to be seen with suspicion with their frequent alleged efforts at bypassing government directives.

Indira Gandhi through the enactment of regulatory laws sought to direct and control the private sector to fulfill economic and social goals. This period, is often characterized as the License - Permit Raj, with its policies to curb big business houses and expand on public sector. Several prominent government commissions, established during this period, documented evidence that big business houses were exerting significant influence on Indian economy, and that they were exploiting growth opportunities through favorable access to finance and government permits. Monopolies and Restrictive Trade Practices Commission was established and the Foreign

24. Malyarov (1983) has given a list of such advisory bodies with business representation.

Exchange Regulation Act (FERA), was enacted. Largest private banks were also nationalized.

At this time, the Indian private sector was dominated by a relatively small number of large family controlled business houses. According to Monopolies Inquiry Commission Report of 1965, there were 75 business houses which controlled almost half of the non-governmental, non-banking assets in the country. In spite of the laws, some of these large private business houses prospered. It is widely believed that many of these business houses used political connections to take business advantages, in spite of the laws so framed. While the policy makers saw the control and regulatory laws to provide for rational allocation of resources and fulfill social goals, private capitalists put their faith in their ability to influence their implementation to benefit from them. Large industrial houses and influential private capitalists manipulated these very regulations and controls to their advantage. The key was in bending the implementation and not in changing the law.[25]

A kind of clandestine partnership emerged between the state and business in India. As Kochanek (1987:1284) points out, the political leadership came to depend very heavily on the system as quid pro quo for securing campaign contributions, and the bureaucracy depended on it for payoffs, employment, power, prestige and patronage. The business community depended on the system to secure and maintain monopoly, protection and guaranteed profitability. In this relationship, it does not come as a surprise that larger business

25. However, Khanna and Talepu (2004) have argued that those business houses that remained in dominant position in spite of these restrictive laws, did so due to their entrepreneurial abilities and not merely due to rent seeking activities.

houses commanded more power and influence.

This was also the period when the potential of being a strong state was seen in terms of state's dominance in the economic sphere and 'its ideological advantage as the presumed defender of collective interest and socialist purposes and as the enemy of private and partial gains' (Rudolph and Rudolph 1987:13). During these early years, Rudolphs point out that the Indian state sought to insulate itself from the exigent pressures of a mobilized society. The result was that support for industrialization and planned development was not so much sought from the people but from the bureaucracy that was seen as the major instrument of implementation of plans. Strengthening bureaucracy was an integral part of the strategy of planned development (Mathur, 1999). Within the Indian federal system where central government was the prime moving agency, system of economic planning and mobilization of financial resources supported by a bureaucratic system in which centralizing tendencies were inherent, local initiative was curbed and a strong control and command system emerged.

However, the Table below shows, that this did not deter the private business companies to grow and expand. During the period between 1951-61 Nehru was the Prime Minister and the relations with private business were far more cordial than when Indira Gandhi succeeded him. Her Prime Ministership lasted through 1984 but she had begun liberalizing in the last three years of her tenure after which Rajiv continued the process.

Industrialization in the Era of Economic Reforms

From the early 1980s, some efforts had begun to loosen the command and control system. Rajiv Gandhi had begun

Growth of Government and non-government companies, 1961-2001. (Average annual growth, per cent)

Period	Government companies		Non-government companies	
	Paid-up capital	Number	Paid-up capital	Number
1951-1961	35.5	11.2	5.4	9.9
1961-1971	14.2	8.3	6.7	1.4
1971-1981	18.7	10.5	7.3	7.5
1981-1991	15.8	3.3	14.3	13.5
1991-2001	7.2	0.8	28.4	9.8

Source: Pederson 2007

initiating some reformist policies that aimed at technological modernization through opening up trade and loosening state regulation. (see Kohli,1989 and Harriss, 1987 for greater details) But the radical change really occurred in 1991 when due to the foreign exchange crisis, India went on to accept the structural adjustment programme offered by the IMF and the World Bank. Licensing system was dismantled, investment was opened up for foreign private investors and trade was liberalized.

Introduction of liberal economic reforms in 1991 was, therefore, of historic significance. The Eighth Five Year Plan (1992-97) that came after India had announced far reaching changes in its economic policies signalled a change in the role of state and government. It began by acknowledging that there is a considerable backlog in the provision of social consumption needs of the people, particularly the poor and for those living in rural areas. It, therefore, called for 'an innovative approach to development which is based on re-examination and reorientation of the role of the government, the harnessing of the latent energies of the people through their involvement in the process of nation building, and the creation of an environment which encourages people's initiative rather than their dependence on the government, and which sets free the forces of growth and modernization.' This reorientation began to get reflected in the way government saw how effective implementation of programmes needed not only strengthening of its own capacity but also a new institutional arrangement that involved other actors in society. The Ninth Plan continued to expand on the reform objectives set by the Eighth Plan. It went on to suggest that 'Our development strategy must be oriented to enabling our broad based and varied private sector to reach its full potential for raising production, creating jobs and raising income levels in society. A vigorous private sector, operating under the discipline of competition and free markets, will encourage efficient use of scarce resources and ensure rapid growth at least cost. Our policies must therefore create an environment which encourages this outcome.'

It is common knowledge that deregulation of the Indian economy was the major thrust of the economic reforms initiated in 1991. It was an effort to create a favourable environment for the private sector to grow and invest in India's growth. The strategy was to prioritise growth as a state goal, support large business houses in achieving this goal and keep labour under control (Kohli, 2006). The institutional framework that was created was to implement this strategy. Unlike during the period of planning, business houses were no more hostile actors out to subvert the goals of the state but partners in achieving them.

This theme found sustenance in the idea of public-private partnership and an effort to search for institutional arrangements that will promote it. In a recent speech, the Prime Minister emphasised that 'a synergy between public support and private initiative can help multiply the productivity of resource utilization.' He went on to say, 'We have been deeply concerned about the efficiency of utilization of public funds, especially in infrastructure development, education and health care. We have been looking for ways of combining our concern for equitable outcomes with our concern for efficient utilization of outlays. PPPs are an effective means of combining these two concerns.'[26] The Eleventh Five Year Plan Approach Paper entitled Towards Faster and More Inclusive Growth spiritedly advocates PPPs as the strategy of development.

Institutional Arrangements for Networks

A consequence of the strategy of forging partnership between state and the private sector was an effort to reach out to consult it in policy formulation. The economic ministries formed Boards that had leading lights of the corporate sector as members and recognised organisation like Federation of Chambers of Commerce and Industry and Confederation of Indian Industry as legitimate forums for political and bureaucratic leadership to interact. The Council on Trade and Industry was created as an institutional framework for partnership between government and business. The Prime Minster emphasised that the partnership flows from our overall strategy of economic reforms. The membership of the Board in 1998 and 2004 when the government changed was as follows:

26 Man Mohan Singh "We'er Off to A Good Start But we have to do more despite fractured mandate..." (Excerpt from an address delivered at the McKinsey meet, *The Times of India* ct. 25, 2007).

Council of Trade and Industry 1998 and 2004

Chairman: Prime Minister

Members 1998	Members 2004
Ratan Tata	Ratan Tata, V Krishnamurthy
Mukesh Ambani	Keshab Mahindra, RP Goenka
RP Goenka	Azim Premji, NR Narayan Murthy
Kumar Mangalam Birla	Rahul Bajaj, Mukesh Ambani
NR Krishnamurthy	Kumaramangalam Birla, J Godrej
Nusli Wadia	Sunil Mittal, Ashok Ganguli
AC Muthiah	Deepak Parekha, MS Banga
PK Mittal	K. Mazumdar Shaw, K Anji Reddy
Dr. Parminder Singh	Venu Srinivasan, SK Munjal
Suresh Krishna	

Member-Secretary:
Principal Secretary to the Prime Minister

According to the government notification in 1998, the Council on Trade & Industry will afford an opportunity for a policy dialogue on important economic issues relevant to Trade and Industry between the Prime Minister and Members of the Council. The Council shall ordinarily meet once in three months on such dates as may be decided by its Chairman. The membership of the Council nearly doubled – from 10 to 18 members – between the two years when the government changed, incorporating many more industrialists rising on the economic horizon. In addition, special sub-groups were also appointed to interact directly with Ministries. Such sub-groups were in the areas like Food & Agro -industries, Management Policy, Infrastructure, Capital Markets and Financial Sector Initiatives, Knowledge-based Industries, Service Industries, Administrative and Legal Simplifications.

The Council of the Ministry of Commerce and Industry,

as the following list of members shows, provided avenues of partnership to other corporate giants.

Members of the Board of Trade
Ministry of Commerce and Industry, 2005

Kumar Mangalam Birla, Aditya Birla Group
Ishaat Hussain, Tata Sons
Baba Kalyani, Bharat Forge
Malvinder Singh, Ranbaxy
Irfan Allana, Allana Sons
Jagdish Khattar, Maruti Udyog
Ravi Raheja, Shoppers Stop
Prashant Ruia, Essar Group
AC Muthiah, SPIC
Harish Neotia, Gujarat Ambuja
Rana Kapoor, Yes Bank
Rama S Deora, Ampray Labs

Associations of industries also provide platforms for the leaders of government and business to interact and deliberate on policy. Federation of Indian Chambers of Commerce and Industry (FICCI) is the rallying point for free enterprise in India. According to its website, 'it has empowered Indian businesses, in the changing times, to shore up their competitiveness and enhance their global reach.' With a nationwide membership of over 1500 corporates and over 500 commerce and business associations, FICCI espouses the shared vision of Indian businesses and speaks directly and indirectly for over 2,50,000 business units. The website further says that 'FICCI maintains the lead as proactive business solution provider through research, interactions at the highest political level and global networking.' Thirty-four specialised committees of FICCI on diverse segments of the economy grapple with sectoral issues on a day-to-day basis to provide solutions to business and suggest pragmatic policies to the Government. Government provides its support to the activities of Joint Business Councils formed by the FICCI with India's trading partners. This is what it calls 'track two diplomacy' to open up new business opportunities for Indian businessmen with overseas investors, technology suppliers, multilateral and bilateral funding agencies. Annual General Meetings of FICCI have been important national economic events. Contemporary developmental issues facing the nation are discussed and debated by the political leadership, business and the academia. These events have helped the Government of India to take stock of the developmental initiatives and to evolve policy corrections based on industry responses.

Confederation of India Industry (CII) is another significant business association with a direct membership of over 5300 companies from the private as well as public sectors, including SMEs and MNCs and indirect membership of over 80,000 organizations from 300 national and regional sectoral associations. Its website says CII catalyses change by working closely with government on policy issues, enhancing efficiency, competitiveness and expanding business opportunities for industry through a range of specialised services and global linkages. With 47 offices in India, 12 overseas and institutional partnerships with 239 counterpart organizations in 101 countries, CII serves as a reference point for industry and international business community. It has paid special attention to its linkages in US and set up an office in Washington in 1995 and has close working relations with organizations such as US Chamber of Commerce, the US-India Business Council, The Aspen Institute and the Brookings Institution. CII has developed strong programmes to brief members of the US

Congess and has sponsored a number of delegations of its members to visit India. As a corollary it also sponsors visits of India parliamentarians to the US. The first delegation went in 2003 and consisted of representatives of various parties. Recently, it sponsored a trip of young parliamentarians to Yale University for an orientation programme.

The Prime Minister and his reform oriented colleagues have played an important role in seeking support from these associations in initiating policies of liberalization. For it must be remembered that Rajiv Gandhi's attempts at deregulation in 1986 onwards faced significant opposition from his own party and bureaucrats and he needed support from business. Sinha (2005) has documented how Rajiv Gandhi played a crucial role in transforming a Confederation of Engineering Industries (CEI) into Confederation of India Industries (CII) that was more broad-based and spoke for the entire industry. Finance Minister ManMohan Singh faced a similar predicament in 1991. He recommended that CII popularize his ideas of economic reform to the opposition in parliament. CII began organizing interactive sessions and this practice has continued. Again, Prime Minister Vajpayee asked CII to invite Benazir Bhutto, Pakistan's former Prime Minister to India when it was politically difficult for him to do so. Similarly, Finance Minister Chidambaram made a request in 2004, 'I would like CII and FICCI to address some of our friends in the Left parties and convince them to increase the Foreign Direct Investment cap.'

The role of CII in influencing public policy is now well recognised and documented (Kochanek 1996; Kohli 2006; Sinha 2005). CII has argued for more open and competitive economy and promoted greater integration of Indian economy with global economy. As quoted by Sinha (2005:15) Tarun

Das, its long time Secretary-General, described 'development as a partnership process between the government and industry and we (CII) are the junior partner of the government.' It has found representations in delegations to WTO and in delegations accompanying the Prime Minister making state visits abroad.[27]

At the highest policy levels an ambience of close partnership between government and business has been created. Senior civil servants are being permitted to go on deputation to work in MNCs or large corporate houses in public interest. Making good use of Section 6(2) of the IAS (Cadre) Rules, 1954, which allows officers to take up assignments outside government, as many as 115 members of the 5,000-odd IAS cadre are holding assignments outside government. At the last count, 64 IAS officers were working with private firms or NGOs while 51 were on foreign assignments, including those with India offices of international organisations. The latest officer to head out is the joint secretary petroleum ministry said to be joining as chief of an oil refinery owned by a corporate major. Meanwhile, to meet the 'shortfall' in the IAS, the government has decided to recruit 'more and more' officers — 110, 120 and 130, respectively in 2008, 2009 and 2010.[28]

At the operational level, public-private-partnerships are

27. Rajiv Gandhi was the first Prime Minister who invited businessmen to accompany him on his foreign trips. On hearing of such inclusion in PM's entourage the Indian Ambassador to the USSR is reported to have telegraphed his displeasure. Rajiv Gandhi told the foreign ministry officials to throw the telegram in the dustbin and proceed with his plans. (Sinha 2005:12)

28. http://timesofindia.indiatimes.com/India/IAS_officers_find_greener_pastures_without_quitting/articleshow/2413135.cms

being promoted to implement infrastructure projects that are not only in transport and power sectors but also in the fields of education and health. Modernization of Indian airports as of construction of national highways, for example, is now being undertaken through public-private partnerships or joint ventures. The need for private participation is primarily to bridge the resources and technology gap and to provide for greater efficiency. Similar reasons to construct highways have been made. Laws have been changed and new institution like National Highway Authority of India has been established to facilitate private sector participation and foreign direct investment.

The Minister of Company Affairs, speaking at a Seminar in 2006, emphasised that the role of the private enterprise in taking the country to higher and higher growth paths, is very important. Government's role is to provide a conducive atmosphere in which business could flourish. He then went on to emphasise the need for freedom of action and initiative by the enterprises as against the pre-reform mindset of viewing the business and its efforts at growth and expansion, with suspicion. We are in the era of PPP.[29]

Democracy in India has remained confined to the phenomenon of election, where once in five years representatives, political parties and formation place their agendas in the public domain. Even on these promised agendas, there is little governance accountability in the interim period. The result is that industrial policies or more directly the issues of public-private partnership find little attention in public discussions.

29. http://www.indlawnews.com/38015ad8fc90dc27e781af47f5446e2d

Conclusions

The new governance structures that have emerged in the era of liberalised economy are making the collaboration between the government and business more open and transparent. But network governance obscures the process and accountability for public policy formulation, decision-making, and execution. Yet, conversely, it opens the door to involvement by a wider range of actors and in ways that are less constrained than those applying to institutions of political authority (Mathur and Skelcher 2007:235). This contradiction can lead to many consequences particularly in a situation where business by default is given a privileged position in a market oriented economy. It will tend dominate all patterns of social and economic transactions. This privileged position can lead to conflicts with government which, in turn, does not want to appear weak in negotiations. As Lindblom (1977:179) points out, inevitably the groups will show hostility towards each other and try to outwit each other to gain upper hand. But these conflicts lie within a range of dispute constrained by their understanding that they together constitute the necessary leadership for the system. This understanding, however, is leading to more and more socially exclusive policies that are not accountable to politically elected authorities. Thus, networks tend to democratise policy-making towards business but carry the risk of insulating it from general democratic structures.

Another characteristic of business, that needs to be strongly underlined, is its continuous pursuit of profit. Profit is a measure of its success and performance. The role of the government is not limited to supporting this pursuit but has larger interests of society that are concerned with its welfare. These concerns may come into conflict with single minded pursuit of profit. Therefore, the issue of networking assumes larger dimensions where the government's purpose is also to temper the business aims and goals. If the state fails in this endeavour, democratic governance suffers. This will inevitably lead to distributional problems that will endanger democracy itself. The close partnership between government and business is being suspect in the eyes of many on particularly two counts: one is of the business houses taking advantage of the favourable relations to promote their own individual interests and the other is the fear of distributional goals being jeopardised by negotiations in these networks.

Network governance is assumed to contribute to the production of public purpose within a certain area. This public purpose is an expression of social vision and the direction the policies should take to achieve this vision. But network governance relies on political and social processes at work in society and they may not be necessarily conducive to the production of public purpose on all occasions (Sorenson and Torfing 2007). There can be cases of governance network failure (Jessop 1998). Increasingly social demands and economic performance are showing a disconnect in India. Democratically elected governments rarely last for more than one term. Such loss at hustings is attributed to what has come to be known as 'incumbency factor' but the reason is really the failure to fulfill the demands of the people that elected them. The classic example has been the defeat of the BJP in 2004 when it ran an election campaign of 'India Shining' based on the achievements in economic growth. It must be realised that increasing number of the poor and the marginalised are now mobilised and participate in elective democracy. There will be a rising tide of demands that growth policies may not be able to satisfy. The government-business networks have also to respond to processes generated by such democratization.

One effort at meeting the above challenge has been the establishment of a plethora of regulatory institutions. The onset of liberal economic reforms in 1991 and the experience of the first few years alerted the policy makers to high risks in a market oriented economy. These risks are not only concerned with market failures but also to the abuse of 'market power by private producers in inherently monopolistic sectors, and to contain the increasingly decentralised and complex transactions in the capital markets leading to risks which lead to systemic collapse' (Bhattacharya and Patel 2005:406). Independent economic regulators were gradually established.

The regulatory institutions are an innovation on the Indian governance scene for they are different from those that were established earlier. These regulators make rules for enterprises to play the game in a level playing field in their respective sectors. A large number of sectoral regulatory agencies have also been established. The first statutory independent regulatory commission Securities and Exchange Board of India (SEBI) was established in 1992. Telecom Regulatory Authority in 2000, Central Electricity Regulatory Commission and many others followed (see Bhattacharya and Patel 2005 for detailed listing).

In addition, India has reviewed the Monopolies and Restrictive Trade Practices Act, 1969 and has enacted the Competition Act, 2002 (the Act) with many innovative features. The Act seeks to repeal the M.R.T.P. Act and to dissolve the M.R.T.P. Commission. The Act through the instrumentality of the Competition Commission of India seeks to prohibit "Anti-Competitive Agreement", "Abuse of Dominant position by an Enterprise " and to regulate certain

"Combinations" which include acquisition of shares, acquiring of control and mergers/amalgamation between and amongst enterprises. The Competition Commission seeks to establish a free market and a 'level playing field' for all the enterprises so the consumer welfare increases. The Competition Commission has been operationalized by an Amendment passed by the Parliament in August 2007.

Though the Competition Commission is mostly driven by complaints from aggrieved parties, there is nothing to prevent the Commission from taking suo moto notice of violations. "Only in the case of mergers, the Commission has an ex-ante role and it could stop a merger, if the deal is likely to have an appreciable adverse effect on competition in the relevant market."[30] "The Competition Commission is not an in-market regulator but sits off-market, while keeping a watchful eye on the goings-on, in case there is any anti-competitive activity," suggests Mr. Dhall, a member of the Commission, "The Competition Commission does not intervene ex-ante in business decisions and it has no power to direct enterprises about how they should conduct their business or set prices. Its role is mainly ex-post; if an enterprise violates any provision of the Competition Act, the Commission has the power to step in and take remedial action" (ibid). It is being increasingly emphasised that the power and functions of the Competition Commission are different from the Monopolies and Restrictive Trade Practices Commission because of change in attitude and acceptance of market driven development.

What is interesting is that regulatory institutions have been created not only to cope with general market failures

30 *The Hindu Business Line*, March 31, 2007 e-paper

but also failures in specific sectors. Competition Commission which seeks to replace the earlier Monopolies and Restrictive Trade Practices Commission rests on the idea that free play of markets will lead to efficient allocation of resources as well as promote competitiveness, hence boosting production and growth. The sectoral regulatory commissions rest on a mutually trusting relationship between the state and the private sector where the interests of state pursuing growth coincide with profit maximizing needs of the private sector (Kohli, 2007:1252-53). The institutionalization of the competition commission has been quite niggardly but networking institutions and regulatory commissions were established pretty early as liberalization proceeded. Business community also had a less interest in free markets but greater attraction in pursuing sectoral opportunities. The government has deemed raising rate of growth as a major goal of development and this coincides with the interest of business groups to maximize their interest. The consequence of such networking is then easy to see.

Whatever the consequences, networks play a significant role in the processes promoting social and economic development. Pingle (2000) has argued that shared understandings are vital for the better functioning of economic decision-making. Shared understandings help overcome bureaucratic resistance and allow the state not to fall prey to social and political interests. Industrialists increase their ability to get necessary infrastructure and collective goods for future growth. As a matter of fact, there is a belief among some observers that 'that the most important factor that changed India over the 1980s had more to do with entrepreneurial attitudes and a belief that rules of the game had changed than with individual policy moves' (Kohli, 2006:1251).[31]

To conclude, it is important to emphasize the context for the functioning of governance networks. This is particularly true in the relationship between government and business. During the Plan era, state was the driver of development and it took upon itself to determine what policies are in public interest. Consultations were held with business but the policies were determined by government. Liberal era from 1991 promotes a market driven economy. Together with liberalization has come the concept of governance that signifies a change in the way public policies are produced. Business also becomes an actor together with government in public policy-making. Thus, policies are negotiated and contested in forums that are both formal and informal. This leads to democratization but also insulation from general elective democratic processes. Such a process of policy-making in which both the actors are committed to a relentless pursuit of economic growth can be risky for the future of democracy in a country where political mobilization of the poor and the marginalized is taking place at a fast pace. Lack of attention towards distribution can create political problems.

Governance networks are embedded in the assumption that the state has the capacity to negotiate with business on equal terms. In contrast to what was happening earlier, the idea of network is based on cooperation and the ability of state to facilitate the role of the market. This role demands state capacity to perform cooperating and enabling functions. The neo-liberal agenda adopted by India was very clear that while the state needs to reduce its scope of activity it also needs to strengthen its capacity in areas that remained with

31 Sen (2007) has argued that this was not necessarily so and changes in macro-policies played a significant role.

it. This capacity is concerned with the strength of state power, or the ability of states to plan and execute policies and to enforce laws cleanly and transparently (Fukuyama 2004). But little attention has been given to this brand of state-building activities. Public administration reforms have been tardy (Mathur 2004). Accountability and coordinating public institutions are in disarray (Kapur and Mehta ed. 2003). In an interview, quoted by Fukuyama (2004:25), Milton Friedman, dean of orthodox free market economists noted recently that a decade earlier he would have three words for countries making transition from socialism: privatise, privatise, privatise. "But I was wrong. It turns out that rule of law is probably more basic than privatization." If state capacity was an important determinant of success of planned economy, it is even more important for a market driven economy.

Chapter VII

Partnerships with Civil Society

In the shift of government to governance, the role of civil society has been very significant. There have been two kinds of strands in this role. One has been that of social movements which has taken the cause of the poor and the marginalized and made the government responsive to their needs through changes in institutions, laws and procedures. The other has been the rise of what have come to be known as Non-Governmental Organizations that have taken upon themselves multifarious roles that includes implementation of governmental programmes. Social movements and Non-Governmental Organizations (NGOs) have carved out new spaces in the political processes and delivering public services.

Civil society as Social Movements

Social movements pose a challenge to the projects, practices, and discourses of the state especially in the sphere of development (Jayal, 2001:137). They start with mobilization for protest and attempt to influence or change government policies or methods of government's project implementation. Among the more well known of such movements has been the Narbada Bachao Andolan, Chipko movement, movement for the recognition of tribal rights in the Forest Bill etc. These movements have been influential in setting policy agenda of government in recent years. Several measures have been undertaken in response to the demands generated in these movements. A very significant achievement, that has the potential of changing the nature of governance in the country has been the move of making information and access to it a right of the citizens. It is this event that we will look into in a little more detail.

Enactment of Right to Information Act is a significant milestone in improving governance in the country. A people's organization in Rajasthan, known as Mazdoor Kisan Shakti Sangathan (MKSS) has been in the vanguard of this struggle. It forced government to respond to the demands of information and accountability. As documented in Roy et.al. (1996), people began to understand that their livelihood, wages and employment depended a great deal on the investments made by the government as a development agency. If these benefits were not coming, then they had the right to know where the investment occurred and how much of it was actually spent. The right to economic well being got translated into right to information. As Roy et.al. (ibid) point out, the struggle became for '*hamara paisa hamara hisab*'. In other words, accountability became a critical issue in the public hearings organised in five blocks of four districts. Four demands were made: transparency of development spending, accountability, sanctity of social audit and redressal. This campaign began in 1994 and gradually gained momentum spreading to most parts of the state. It reached a level where assurances had to be provided by the Chief Minister.

The essence of the campaign that steamrollered into a movement for right to information was the *jan sunwai* (public hearing) where villagers assembled to testify whether the public works that have been met out of the expenditures certified by the government actually exist or not. The first *Jan sunwai* was held in a village of Kot Kirana in 1994. Since then they have caught the imagination of the MKSS that has held them at several places. Beawar was the scene of a major event in April 1996. It was followed by a 40-day dharna in which activists were fed and sheltered by the public. Another 53-day dharna was organized at Jaipur (see Bunker Roy, *The Asian Age* 30 May 2001). The Rajasthan government responded reluctantly but the Chief Minister ultimately announced that the people had the right to demand and receive details of expenditure on development works in their villages.

Three months after the event in Beawar, politicians, jurists, former bureaucrats, academics and others joined in demanding right to information legislation at a conference in New Delhi. A committee under the chairmanship of Justice PB Sawant was authorised to draft a model bill. The central government too came under pressure to introduce legislation in the Parliament that could be followed by the states.

Government of India set up a Working Group on Right to Information and Promotion of Open and Transparent Government in 1997. The terms of reference of the Group included the examination of feasibility and need to introduce a full fledged Right to Information Act so as to meet the needs of open and responsive government. The Working Group placed its tasks within the broad framework of democracy and accountability and emphasised, 'democracy means choice and a sound and informed choice is possible only on the basis of knowledge'(Working Group Report, 1997:3). It also argued that transparency and openness in functioning have a cleansing effect on the operations of public agencies and approvingly quoted the saying that sunlight is the best disinfectant.

The Working Group accepted the following broad

principles to the formulation of the legislation:

a) disclosure of information should be the rule and secrecy the exception;
b) the exceptions should be clearly defined;
c) There should be an independent mechanism for adjudication of disputes between the citizens and public authorities.

A draft bill was put to public debate and a Freedom of Information Act was finally placed on the statute book in 2003. The main weakness of this Act was that it did not acknowledge right to information of the people. Consequently, it provided for appeals only within the government bodies. It barred jurisdiction of the Courts and did not ensure any appeal with any independent body (GuhaRoy, 2006:10). The new government coming in 2004 enacted a Right to Information Act in 2005 which recognized citizen's access to information as a right. It provided for Central and State Information Commissions as appellate authorities and laid down penalties for refusal to accept applications for information and malafide intention to deny request for information.

Since the availability of the right to information, citizens have used it extensively. Several voluntary agencies have emerged that help the people to use this right to solve their problems. Media has also used it to make people aware of decisions that had remained within the covers of official file. The right to information has also emerged as an important tool in the hands of citizens for redressal of their grievances. The government has initiated corrective action in many cases where it has been brought to light that patent injustice was done.

Civil Society as Non-Governmental Organizations

Organized voluntary action has a long history in India. In the first half of the twentieth century, the major factor in the growth of voluntary agencies was the mass mobilization and political campaigns undertaken during the independence struggle. Gandhi's 'constructive work' activities that began from the 1920s had economic and social reform dimensions, which also influenced the growth of voluntary agencies. In the post-independence period, many of these Gandhian organizations were led by public figures who did not (or could not) join the ruling Congress government. These groups worked closely with the government for the development of handicrafts and cottage industries, credit and other cooperatives and educational institutions. Official institutions such as the Central Social Welfare Board, Khadi and Village Industries Commission and People's Action Development India were established in 1950s and 1960s to promote and fund a large number of voluntary social work organizations of this kind (Khan, 1997:5). In the decades beginning 1960s, there was further growth of such organizations with educated and professional people beginning to join voluntary action in large numbers. The non-governmental organizations (NGOs) that came into being in this way kept close linkage and touch with professional research institutions like the Tata Institute of Social Sciences, Institute of Rural Management, Indian Social Institute, Center for Women's Studies etc. Good performance of several NGOs brought recognition to individuals who headed them and government began to incorporate them in official agencies. Sanjit (Bunker) Roy of the Social Work and Research Center (SWRC), Tilonia, became adviser to the Planning Commission during Rajiv Gandhi's tenure as Prime Minister; Ela Bhatt of SEWA

Ahmedabad was nominated as member of the Upper House of Parliament and also appointed Chairperson of National Commission on Self-Employed Women.

The Eighth Five-Year Plan (1992-97) re-examined and re-oriented the role of government by laying considerable stress on strengthening of people's participatory institutions. It suggested that it is necessary to make development a people's movement. The Plan went on to indicate that in areas like education (especially literacy), health, family planning, land improvement, efficient land use, minor irrigation, watershed management, recovery of wastelands, afforestation, animal husbandry, dairy, fisheries, sericulture, etc. a lot can be achieved by creating people's institutions that are accountable to the community. In contrast to the earlier Second Five Year Plan, which stated that 'the state had to take on heavy responsibilities as the principal agency speaking for and acting on behalf of the community as whole', the Eighth Plan made a strong plea for greater role of the voluntary sector (Mathur: 1996, 24-40). Three Five Year Plans later, the Approach Paper to the Eleventh Five Year Plan, has explicitly recognized that 'many civil society organizations have a proven track record of implementing programmes at the grass-roots level and they have shown impressive results in this area.'

In May 2007, the Planning Commission announced National Policy for the Voluntary Sector. This Policy is an expression of 'a commitment to encourage, enable and empower an independent, creative and effective voluntary sector, with diversity in form and function, so that it can contribute to the social, cultural and economic advancement of the people of India.' This policy further 'recognizes the important role that the voluntary sector has to play in various areas and affirms the growing need for collaboration with the voluntary sector by the Government, as well as by the private sector, at the local, provincial and national levels.' The policy lays down the following objectives:

a. To create an enabling environment for VOs that stimulates their enterprise and effectiveness, and safeguards their autonomy;
b. To enable VOs to legitimately mobilize necessary financial resources from India and abroad;
c. To identify systems by which the Government may work together with VOs, on the basis of the principles of mutual trust and respect, and with shared responsibility; and,
d. To encourage VOs to adopt transparent and accountable systems of governance and management.

The Policy emphasizes partnership of government with the voluntary organizations and recognizes three instruments of partnerships: viz., (i) consultation, through a formal process of interaction at the Centre, State and District level; (ii) strategic collaboration to tackle complex interventions where sustained social mobilization is critical over the long term; and (iii) project funding through standard schemes. The policy then lays down the measures that government will take to achieve these objectives.

Government is promoting the role of what it calls voluntary organizations or NGOs in governance through the above policy. What follows is a brief account of some illustrations of the way the government-civil society partnership is evolving in India in the social sector.

Health Sector Reform

There is a widespread belief that neither the government by itself nor the private sector can provide the needed health services to the people. What is required is cooperative action with other actors of the society. For such cooperative action, new institutions are required and thus the idea of public-private partnership was born. While public sector includes all agencies under the government's budgetary control, private sector includes both profit and non-profit agencies. The non-profit agencies are the NGOs. There are many forms of partnerships but contracting seems to be the dominant form.

Currently several private partnership initiatives are under implementation in the states of India. The scope of these initiatives span disease surveillance; purchase and distribution of drugs in bulk; contracting specialists for high risk pregnancies; national disease control programs; social marketing; adoption and management of primary health centers; co-location of private facilities (blood banks, pharmacy); subsidies and duty exemptions; joint ventures; contracting medical education and training; engaging private sector consultants; pay clinics; discount vouchers; self-regulation; R&D investments; telemedicine; health cooperatives; and accreditation. Among the 16 case studies of public- private partnership undertaken by Venkatraman and Bjorkman (2007) eight are those of public sector and NGOs. Their analysis suggests that the most successful partnerships have been with NGOs in spite of the fact many terms and conditions have not been as favourable to them as to 'for profit' sector. Poor patients seem to have benefited from the partnership arrangements. The NGOs have also succeeded in taking over management of hospitals in partnership with government.. For example, in the case of Arpana Swasthya Kendra, the Municipal Corporation of Delhi (MCD) had built a maternity health centre through funds from the World Bank's India Population Project-VIII but the building was not operational due to non-deployment of staff. An NGO that had been working in the slum community approached the IPP-VIII project director in MCD with a request to let the NGO manage the health centre. The project director worked hard to convince the political leaders and administrative heads of the corporation, eventually obtaining their approval for a proposal to transfer the health centre to the NGO under a fixed-term agreement.

Rogi Kalyan Samitis[32]

Another example of a community based management of hospitals in partnership with government comes from Madhya Pradesh. The Rogi Kalyan Samiti emerged out of the way the threat of plague was handled by Indore city in 1994. Citizens undertook to clean up the city as preemptive action. A large number of people volunteered to do so but discovered that the major city hospital was itself infested with rats and required major clean up. The District Collector and the state government offered support and the clean-up, though being a gigantic operation, was a great success. This exercise led to the demand for the improvement of the functioning of the hospital. A new structure with citizens representatives came into being providing for more participative management of the hospital. Thus was born the Rogi Kalyan Samiti.

In 1996, the state government issued a formal government order institutionalizing the RKS model throughout the state. The Samitis are registered under the Madhya Pradesh Societies Registration Act 1973, with the mandate to manage the hospital and the powers to mobilize additional finances, apply them to local needs, hire staff on

32. Based on Sadanandan and Shiv Kumar (2006).

contract basis and carry out other activities to improve hospital services. Typically, the General Body consists of elected representatives, government officials, medical professionals, social workers and citizens. This kind of an arrangement has had considerable influence on health reform. Institutions such as Hospital Development Society in Kerala, the Medical Relief Society in Rajasthan, Chikitsa Prabhandan Committee in Uttaranchal and Aspatal Kalyan Samiti appear to have roots in the experiment tried at Indore.

NGOs in Education

Like in health, government performance in providing education for all has not been adequate. Without going into actual data, it is now widely recognized that the spread of education in the rural areas and among the poor and the deprived has been disappointing and in most areas where education has reached its quality has not been of high standard. NGOs play an important role in contributing to filling the gaps in the efforts of the government. There are a very large number of NGOs working in the field of education. A number of them are locally based, while many others have a national reach. In a recent World Bank study, Jagannathan (2001) examines the importance of GO-NGO partnerships to hasten universal primary education and to enrich its quality. It presents case studies of 6 NGOs working in different spheres of elementary education and explores the path they have taken to scale up and replicate their models in the Government system.[33] The NGOs surveyed are: M. Venkatarangaiya Foundation, Pratham Mumbai Education Initiative, Bodh Shiksha Samiti, Rishi Valley Rural Education

33. The profiles of the NGOs are extracted from this study.

Centre, Eklavya and the Centre for Education Management and Development (CEMD). Bodh, Pratham and MV Foundation have a strong agenda for social activism whereas Rishi Valley, Eklavya and CEMD are professional resource agencies. The expansion of the activities of Bodh and CEMD is relatively on a smaller scale than that of the others.

The MV Foundation (MVF), a private, charitable Trust in Andhra Pradesh, has developed a model that uses education as a means of tackling child labour. One of the key features of MVF's intervention is the reliance on the formal, regular Government schools to provide for the education of hitherto working children. MVF has influenced the larger educational scenario by collaborating closely with Government schools. MVF's work has been instrumental in making the Government of Andhra Pradesh revamp several thousand NFE centres in the State into day centres, operating in much the same way as formal schools do, or as motivation centres in the villages, whereas earlier they were running evening classes. MVF has trained NFE instructors to play the role of education activists rather than act as poor substitutes for teachers. On the one hand, MVF's activities exposes the severe limitations of the traditional NFE program and, on the other hand, reaffirms the role of the formal school in making even the most difficult group literate. The Government of Andhra Pradesh has also made a strong policy pronouncement for the eradication of child labour.

The Pratham Mumbai Education Initiative started using early childhood education as a means to universalize primary education when it started its work in the city of Mumbai. Pratham, a public charitable trust, began with an UNICEF initiative, which aimed to send all children to school in Mumbai City. Addressing the total lack of pre-school facilities for the urban deprived in Mumbai, a few balwadis (pre-school centres) were started in 1995. Pratham now runs nearly 3000 balwadis in the slums of Mumbai, catering to more than half of Mumbai's needs. Pratham's defined objective is to ensure that all children in the age group of 3-10 years are enrolled in pre-school centres or primary schools. Pratham, like the MV Foundation, is seeking to make the Government education network take cognizance of the schooling needs of the poor and be responsive to the communities.

Although Pratham's program currently lies predominantly in pre-school education facilities in the slums of Mumbai, it operates from resource centers within a number of Municipal Schools in Mumbai. Pratham's stance is that it is impossible to universalize primary education without working with Municipal Schools.

Bodh Shiksha Samiti began its work in the 1980s in the slums of Jaipur, Rajasthan, to provide appropriate education to the children of socially marginalized groups. To provide schooling to slum children, Bodh recruited motivated, under qualified youth and put them through intensive teacher training. Bodh also believes in the crucial importance of collaborating with the Government schooling system in order to have a larger influence.

The Rishi Valley Rural Education Centre (RVREC) was set up in the early 1980s with the objective of catering to the education needs of the rural countryside of Andhra Pradesh, adjoining the well-known Rishi Valley Public School. It has experimented with schooling through alternative to traditional textbook method. Eklavya, in Madhya Pradesh started with developing innovative curriculum, teaching methodologies and educational materials for science teaching. It has established an effective collaboration with government school system.

The Centre for Education Management and Development (CEMD) is essentially a resource centre and started with the notion that an effective school requires a strong management backing to innovations and experiments. It was recognized that school improvement programs needed to encompass effective financial and human resource management and leadership for curricular and classroom change. A major weakness identified by CEMD was that school heads in India received practically no training to handle administrative and management functions. CEMD was founded with the objective of developing school improvement programs with a "whole-school-management" approach. This emerged from the felt need for a "systems approach" to improving school quality and to institutionalize the process of change and reform. After working with private schools with poor resources that cater to the socio economically disadvantaged, CEMD is now involved in transposing its model to a sample of Delhi Government schools.

As can be seen from above, NGOs have reached out to neglected communities and experimented with innovative approaches to improve quality of education. They have also attempted to work with government school system realizing that the problem is too large to be tackled by the NGOs alone.

The few illustrations above show how partnerships are being built up with NGOs to pursue aims of development. During the regime of UPA government, (2004-) a National Advisory Council under the chairpersonship Mrs. Sonia Gandhi was formed. This Council was meant to monitor the implementation of the Common Minimum Programme agreed to by the parties in the coalition. The Council included representatives of NGOs and some non-officials. This was the first recognition of the role of the NGOs in governance at the highest level. Currently (2007), however, this Council is in abeyance with the Chairperson having resigned due to political reasons.

Chapter VIII

Quest for Good Governance

As we conclude our brief survey of the movement of government to governance, the emphasis of governance on the efficacy of institutions and democracy and participation needs to be reiterated. While it is accepted that governance seeks to dilute the monopoly of political institutions in resolving societal problems and actively seeks other actors to play this role jointly or independently, the need to coordinate the roles of many players still remains. This coordination and coherence among a wide disparate array of actors with different objectives and interests can only be brought about by state and its institutions.

In this emerging web of institutions, it should not be believed that the state is ineffective. It still remains a pivotal institution. Without state playing its role and the capacity to do so, the network of institutions cannot perform functions they have been set up for. State is the source of laws and democracy legitimizes them. Laws are meant to resolve conflicts and maintain harmony in society. Together with making laws, state is the only agency that can enforce them for it has the monopoly of the use of coercive power. Thus, a democratic state is based on rule of law and the critical question is its capacity to act on this basis. This capacity does not stem from coercion alone but from legitimacy. Governance, with its extensive participative institutions, will presumably be in a better position, to provide legitimacy than a state-centric governance. Participative institutions help the state to enforce laws effectively and transparently. This is what the move towards governance does.

However, state capacity is not only a function of legitimacy. It is also a function of the performance of institutions and their ability to rise up to the tasks allocated to them. Bureaucracy is the most important instrument of implementation of public policies. It has not yet adjusted to the new paradigm of governance and continues to act in a mode reminiscent of an era gone by. Innumerable committees and commissions have been set to reform it but the elephant has moved very slowly. This is one of the foremost challenges of good governance in India today. Unless the government institutions themselves have the capacity and capability for high performance, their ability to negotiate in forums of partnerships and networks with other actors will be weakened considerably.

In this surge for creating new institutions, existing institutions appear to get neglected. Instead of committing greater time and re-examining the way the Parliament can perform its core functions of accountability and legislation more effectively, solutions like establishing Standing Committees can turn out to be poor substitutes of debate and contestation which is an essential part of democracy. Similarly, fast track courts cannot ultimately take care of the ills of the criminal justice system nor can out-sourcing take care of bureaucratic ills. Paradoxically, weak institutions have also to demonstrate some strength in order to survive and justify their existence. A tendency then develops to encroach on the functions of another. This is amply demonstrated by the frequent squabbles among the Parliament, the Supreme Court and bureaucracy.

The major challenge that India faces is building state capacity. And state capacity stems from effective institutions. Experience all over the world demonstrates that institutions cannot be imported and are culturally specific. This requires home-grown policies and strategies to make state institutions more effective. Market based solutions to problems of public systems may not be possible in all jurisdictions or be effective in serving social purpose. Moves towards NGOs and community-based organizations are important for participation but create their own problems of accountability. These also have to be addressed.

Over the years, after independence, there has been a gradual decline in the effectiveness of institutions of accountability. It is now being increasingly left to civil society to raise issues connected with financial probity and administrative responsibility. Right to Information has attempted to fill in the accountability gap and so also Public Interest Litigation has helped aggrieved groups to fight the arbitrariness of the state. Getting such redressal is not easy and continues to be a struggle against state mechanisms. Even decentralization after the Constitutional Amendments has been an uphill task. However, in face of weaknesses in other institutions of accountability, Right to Information is proving to be a strong instrument against corruption and holding public officials accountable for their public functions. Perhaps, it is now the most important step in the quest for good governance.

Thus, the movement from government to governance is not merely a task of creating new institutions but also that of refurbishing old ones. It is also of accepting that state has to be strengthened to play a new role. It is also for the civil society to accept that democracy is not going to polls every five years but being vigilant and monitoring institutional performance and holding them accountable throughout these years.

References

Agarwal Arun, 2005, 'Indian Parliament' in Kapur Mehta, ed., *Public Institutions in India,* op.cit.

Alexander, PC., 1991, *My Years with Mrs Gandhi,* Vision Books, New Delhi.

Ananthpur, Kripa, 2004, *Rivalry or Synergy? Formal and Informal Local Governance in Rural India,* IDS Working Paper 226, Institute of Development Studies, Sussex.

Austin, Granville, 2003, *Working a Democratic Constitutions A History of the Indian Experience,* Oxford University Press, New Delhi.

Bandopadhyay, D., 2003, 'Twelfth Finance Commission and Panchayat Finances' *Economic and Political Weekly,* xxxviii, 23, June 7, 2242-3.

Banik Dan, 2001, 'The Transfer Raj: Indian Civil Servants on the Move', *The European Journal Development Research,* 13, 1, June 2001, 106-134.

Bardhan, Pranab, 1996, 'Decentralized Development', *Indian Economic Review,* xxxi, 2, 139-56.

Bardhan, Pranab, K., 1998, *Political Economy of Development in India,* Oxford University Press, New Delhi.

Behar, A. (2003), "Madhya Pradesh: Experiment with Direct Democracy, Time for Reappraisal", *Economic and Political Weekly,* 17 May.

Behar, Amitabh and Yamini Aiyar, 2003, 'Networks of Panchayat Women: Civil Society Space for Political Action', *Economic and Political Weekly,* xxxviii,47, 4936-40.

Bhagwati, Jagdish, 1995, *India in Transition,* Clarendon Press, Oxford.

Bhambhri, CP, 1998, 'Of a Partisan, Self-Serving Bureaucracy', *The Pioneer* (Delhi edition), 23 September.

Bhattacharya, Saugata and Urjit R. Patel, 2005, 'New Regulatory Institutions in India: White Knights or Trojan Horses' in Devesh Kapur and Pratap Bhanu Mehta (eds) 2005 *Public Institutions in India Performance and Design*, Oxford University Press, Delhi.

Braibanti, Ralph, 1966, Transnational Inducement of Administrative Reform: A Survey of Scope and Critique of Issues in Montgomery John D. and William J. Siffin (ed), 1966, *Approaches to Development Politics, Administration and Change*, McGraw Hill, New York.

Chaturvedi, MK, 1971, 'Commitment in Civil Service', *Indian Journal of Public Administration,* xvii, 1, 40-46.

Chatterjee, Partha, 1998, 'Development Planning and the Indian State', in Byres, TJ. 1998. (ed.) *The State, Development Planning and Liberalization in India*, Oxford University Press, Delhi.

Das, SK, 2005, Institutions of Internal Accountability in Kapoor and Mehta ed. *Op.cit.*

Das, SK. 1998, *Civil Service Reform and Structural Adjustment*, Oxford University Press, New Delhi.

Dutt Report, 1969, *Report of the Industrial Licensing Policy Enquiry Committee*, Main Report, Government of India, New Delhi .

Deshpande, S.V. and G.B.V. Murthy, 2002, "Pressures from Below: Decentralised Governance in Karnataka", *Economic and Political Weekly*, 4 May.

Dubhashi, PR, 1971, 'Committed Bureaucracy,' *Indian Journal of Public Administration,* xvii, 1, 33-39.

Fernandes, Aurleno, 2003, 'Aggrandizer Government and Local Governance', *Economic and Political Weekly*, xxxviii, 27, July 5, 2873-79.

Fukuyama, Francis, 2004, *State Building Governance and World Order in the Twenty-First Century,* Profile Books, London.

Ghatak, Maitreesh and Ghatak Maitreya, 2002, 'Recent Reforms in the Panchayat System in West Bengal Towards Greater

Participatory Governance', *Economic and Political Weekly*, xxxvii, 1, 45-58.

Government of India,1978, *Report of the Committee on Panchayati Raj Institutions* (Chairman Asok Mehta), New Delhi.

Government of India, 1997, *Report of the Working Group on Right to Information and Promotion of Open and Transparent Government*, New Delhi.

Government of India, 2002, *National Human Development Report*, Planning Commission, New Delhi.

Government of India, 2006, *The State of the Panchayats A Mid-Term Review and Appraisal 22 November 2006*, Ministry of Panchayati Raj, New Delhi, vol. III.

Guha, Ramchandra, 2007, *India After Gandhi The History of the World Largest Democracy*, Picador, New Delhi.

Guha Roy, Jaytilak, 2006, *Right to Information Initiatives and Impact*, Indian Institute of Public Administration, New Delhi

Grindle, Merlee S., 2004, 'Good Enough Governance: Poverty Reduction and Reform in Developing Countries', *Governance*, An International Journal of Policy, Administration and Institutions 17, 4, October, 525-548.

Hajer, Maarten A. and H. Wagenaar (ed), 2003, *Deliberative Policy Analysis Understanding Governance in Network Society*, Cambridge University Press, Cambridge.

Harriss, John, 1987, 'The State in Retreat: Why has India Experienced Such Half-Hearted Liberalization in the 1980s', *IDS Bulletin*, 18 4:29-36.

Hazari, R.K., 1966, *The Structure of the Corporate Private Sector: A Study of Concentration, Ownership and Control*, Asia Publishing House, Bombay.

Hirst, Paul A., 2000, 'Democracy and Governance' in Pierre (ed), 2000, *Debating Governance*, Oxford University Press, Oxford.

Isaac, TM Thomas, 2001, 'Campaign for Democratic Decentralization in Kerala', *Social Scientist*, Sept-Oct. pp.8-47.

Isaac, TM Thomas and Richard W Franke, 2001 (rev.ed.), *Local*

Democracy and Development People's Campaign for Decentralised Planning in Kerala, Leftword Books New Delhi.

Jagannathan, Shanti, 2001, 'The Role of Non-Governmental Organizations in Primary Education A Study of Six NGOs in India', Policy Research Working Paper 3530, The World Bank Institute, The McNamara Fellowship Programme, The World Bank, Washington,

Jain, RB, 1985, 'Electronics Policy and Indian Parliament', *Indian Journal of Public Administration*, April-June pp.239-74.

Jain, RB, 2000, 'New Directions in Administrative Reforms in India', in Vinod Mehta (ed), *Reforming Administration in India*, Indian Council of Social Science Research and Har Anand Publications, New Delhi.

Jayal, Niraja Gopal, 2007, 'Whatever Happened to the Argumentative Indian?', *Seminar*, January, no. 569 24-27.

Jayal, Niraja Gopal, 2001, 'Introduction' in Niraja G. Jayal and Sudha Pai (ed.), *Democratic Governance in India*, Sage Publications, New Delhi.

Jenkins, Rob, 1999, *Democratic Politics and Economic Reform in India*, Cambridge University Press Cambridge.

Jessop, B., (1998), 'The Rise of Governance and the Risks of Failure. The Case of Economic Development', *International Social Science Journal*, Vol. 50, no. 155, pp. 29-45.

Joseph, KP, 2000, 'Budget Deficits Are Forever', *Economic and Political Weekly*, XXXV,34, 2998-3001.

Kapur, Devesh and Pratap Bhanu Mehta (eds.), 2003, *Public Institutions in India Performance and Design*, Oxford University Press, Delhi.

Kashyap, Subhash, 2000, 'Institutions of Governance: The Parliament, the Government and the Judiciary', in VA Pai Panandiker (ed.), *Problems of Governance in South Asia*, Centre for Policy Research and Konark Publishers, New Delhi, pp.89-154.

Khanna, Tarun and Palepu Krishna, 2004, 'The Evolution of Concentrated Ownership in India Broad Patterns and a

History of The Indian Software Industry', Working Paper 10613 http://www.nber.org/papers/w10613 National Bureau of Economic Research, Cambridge Mass.

Khilnani, Sunil, 1997, *The Idea of India*, Hamish Hamilton, London.

Kochanek, Stanley, A., 1987, 'Briefcase Politics in India The Congress Party and the Business Elite', *Asian Survey*, 27, 12, December pp. 1278-1301.

Kochanek, Stanley, 1996, 'Liberalization and Business Lobbying in India', *Pacific Affairs*, 34, 3, 155-173.

Kohli, Atul, 1989, 'The Politics of Economic Liberalization in India', *World Development,* 17, 3,:305-328.

Kohli, Atul, 2006, 'Politics of Economic Growth in India 1980-2005', *Economic and Political Weekly*, April 1 1251-59 and April 8 2006 Part II 1361-1370.

Kohli, Atul, 1990, *Democracy and Discontent India's Growing Crisis of Governability*, Cambridge University Press, Cambridge.

Krishna, A., 2002, *Active Social Capital*, Columbia University Press, New York.

Leftwich, Adrian, 1994, 'Governance, the State and Politics of Development', *Development and Change*, 25:363-386.

Lindblom, Charles, E, 1977, *Politics and Markets The World's Political-Economic Systems*, Ambika Publications (Indian reprint), New Delhi.

Maheshwari, SR, 2004, 'Administrative Reform in India Past, Present and Future Prospects', *CPR Occasional Paper Series*, Centre for Policy Research, New Delhi.

Manor, James, 1994, 'The Prime Minister and the President', in J. Manor (ed.) *Nehru to the Nineties: The Changing Office of Prime Minister in India*, Hurst & Co. London, pp. 115-137.

Manor, James, 1999, *The Political Economy of Democratic Decentralization*, The World Bank, Washington DC.

Manor, James 2005 The Presidency in Kapur and Mehta **op.cit.**

Malyarov, O.V., 1983, *The Role of the State in the Socio-Economic Structure of India*, Vikas, New Delhi.

Marathe, SS, 1989 (rev.ed.), *Regulation and Development: India's*

Policy Experience of Controls over Industry, Sage Publications, New Delhi.

Mathew, George, 2000, *Panchayati Raj in India – An Overview in Status of Panchayati Raj in States and Union Territories of India 2000*, Institute of Social Sciences and Concept Publishing Company, New Delhi.

Mathew, George, 2001, 'Panchayat Elections – Dismal Record', *Economic and Political Weekly*, January 20.

Mathur, Kuldeep and Niraja Jayal, 1992, *Drought Policy and Politics The Need for a Long Term Perspective*, Sage Publications New Delhi.

Mathur, Kuldeep, 1991, 'Bureaucracy in India: Development and Pursuit of Self Interest', *Indian Journal of Public Administration*, xxxvi, 4.

Mathur, Kuldeep, 1999, 'Strengthening Bureaucracy State and Development in India', *Indian Social Science Review*, 1, 1, January-June, pp 7-28.

Mathur, Kuldeep, 2004, 'Administrative Reform in India Policy Prescriptions and Outcomes' in Surendra Munshi and Biju Paul Abraham (ed.), *Good Governance, Democratic Societies and Globalization*, Sage Publications, New Delhi, pp. 214-231.

Mathur, Navdeep and Chris Skelcher, 2007, 'Evaluating Democratic Performance: Methodologies for Assessing the Relationships between Network Governance and Citizens', *Public Administration Review*, 67, 2, March/April 228-237.

Mehta, Pratap Bhanu, 2005, 'India's Judiciary:The Promise of Uncertainty' in Kapur and Mehta *op.cit.*

Nayar, Baldev Raj, 1998, 'Business and India's Economic Policy Reforms', *Economic and Political Weekly*, 33 (38):2453-2468.

Pedersen, Jorgen, 2007, 'The Transformation of Indian Business: from Passive Resisters to Active Promoters of Globalization', Paper prepared for Sixth Pan-European Conference on International Relations, Italy, 12-15 September available at http://www.sgir.org/archive/turin/uploads/Pedersen-

The%20transformation%20of%20Indian%20business.pdf

Pierre, Jon (ed), 2000, *Debating Governance*, Oxford University Press, Oxford.

Pingle, Vibha, 2000, *Rethinking the Developmental State: India's Industry in Comparative Perspective*, Oxford University Press, Delhi,

Piramal, Gita, 1998, *Business Legends*, Viking, Penguin India, New Delhi.

Peters, B. Guy, 2001, *The Future of Governing*, University Press of Kansa, Lawrence Kansas.

Potter, David, 1986, *India's Political Administrators*, Clarendon Press, Oxford.

Rani, P Geetha, 1999, 'State Finance Commissions and Rural Local Bodies: Devolution of Resources', *Economic and Political Weekly*, XXXIV, 25, June 19-25.

Rao, M. Govinda and Nirvikar Singh, 2005, 'India's Federal Institutions and Economic Reform' in Kapur and Mehta, 2005, *Public Institutions in India Performance and Design*, op.cit.

Rhodes, RAW, 1997, *Understanding Governance Policy Networks, Governance, Reflexivity and Accountability*, Open University Press, Buckingham.

Roy, Aruna, Nikhil Dey and Shanker Singh, 2001, 'Demanding Accountability' *Seminar*, April.

Rubinoff, Arthur, G, 1996, 'India's New Subject-Based Parliamentary Committees' *Asian Survey*, xxxvi, 7, July 723-738.

Rudolph, Lloyd I. and Susanne Hoeber Rudolph, 1987, *In Pursuit of Lakshmi: The Political Economy of the Indian State*, The University of Chicago Press, Chicago and London.

Rudolph, LI and Rudolph SI, 2001, 'Iconisation of Chandrababu Sharing Sovereignty in India's Federal Market Economy', *Economic and Political Weekly*, May 5:1541-1552.

Sadanandan, Rajeev and N. Shiv Kumar, 2007, 'Rog Kalyan Samitis: A Case Study of Hospital Reforms in Madhya Pradesh' in Vikram K. Chand (ed.), *Reinventing Public Service*

Delivery in India Selected Case Studies, The World Bank and Sage Publications, New Delhi.

Santha, EK, 2002, Four Dalit panchayats Prevented Again from Going to Elections, *Panchayati Raj Update,* October p.1953.

Sarkaria Commission, 1989, *Report on Centre-State Relations*, Government of India, New Delhi.

Sathe, SP, 2003, *Judicial Activism in India,* Oxford University Press, Delhi.

Seminar Committed Civil Service: A Symposium, 1973, 168, August.

Sen, Kunal, 2007, 'Why did the Elephant Start to Trot? India's growth Acceleration Re-Examined', *Economic and Political Weekly*, XLII, 43, October 27-November 2, 37-48.

Sinha, Aseem, 2005, 'Understanding the Rise and Transformation of Business Collective Action in India' *Business and Politics*, 7,2:Article 2.

Sharma, Kumud, 1998, 'Transformative Politics: Dimensions of Women's Participation in Panchayati Raj', *Indian Journal of Gender Studies,* 5,1.

Sharma, Rashmi, 2003, 'Kerala's Decentralization Idea in Practice', *Economic and Political Weekly*, xxxviii, 36, 3832-50.

Spangenburg, Bradford, 1976, *British Bureaucracy in India Status, Policy and the ICS, in the Late* 19th *Century,* Manohar Book Service, Delhi.

Surya, Prakash A, 1995, *What Ails India Parliament An Exhaustive Diagnosis*, Indus, An Imprint of HarperCollins Publishers India, New Delhi.

Thakurdas, Purshotomdas, et al., 1944, *Memorandum Outlining a Plan of Economic Development for India*, (Bombay Plan), Penguin Books, Hammondsworth:

United Nations Development Programme undated, *Decentralization in India Challenges and Opportunities,* Human Resources Development Centre Discussion Paper Series – 1, New Delhi.

Venkataramiah, ES, 1997, 'MPs Constituency Development Scheme: Assaulting the Constitution', *Indian Express.*

Febrauary 13 Delhi Edition.

Venkat Raman, A and J.W.Bjorkman, 2006, 'Public/Private Partnership in Health Care Services in India', in *India's Development: Even or Uneven? Reflections on Development Theory and Prcatice*, Indo-Dutch Programme on Alternatives in Development (IDPAD), end-phase symposium proceedings, 1-3 November, Hyderabad, Pg. 73-98.

World Bank, 1989, *Sub-Saharan Africa: From Crisis to Sustainable Growth*, World Bank, Washington DC .

World Bank, 1992, *Governance and Development*, Washington DC World Bank.

Printed at: JJ Imprints Pvt. Ltd. Noida.